Commission of the European Communities

EUROPEAN ECONOMY

Reports and Studies

Directorate-General for Economic and Financial Affairs

1993
Number 6

CANCELLED

E3.3b

E.I.U.

© ECSC-EEC-EAEC, Brussels • Luxembourg, 1993

Printed in Belgium

The economic
and financial situation
in Denmark

This study was prepared under the sole responsibility of the Directorate-General for Economic and Financial Affairs, and submitted to the Economic Policy Committee which discussed it in September 1993. The forecast data included in this report are based on the EC-Commission forecast from June 1993.

Abbreviations and symbols used

Member States

B	Belgium
DK	Denmark
D	Germany
WD	West Germany
GR	Greece
E	Spain
F	France
IRL	Ireland
I	Italy
L	Luxembourg
NL	The Netherlands
P	Portugal
UK	United Kingdom
EUR 9	European Community excluding Greece, Spain and Portugal
EUR 10	European Community excluding Spain and Portugal
EUR 12 –	European Community, 12 Member States including West Germany
EUR 12 +	European Community, 12 Member States including Germany

Currencies

ECU	European currency unit
BFR	Belgian franc
DKR	Danish krone
DM	German mark (Deutschmark)
DR	Greek drachma
ESC	Portuguese escudo
FF	French franc
HFL	Dutch guilder
IRL	Irish pound (punt)
LFR	Luxembourg franc
LIT	Italian lira
PTA	Spanish peseta
UKL	Pound sterling
USD	US dollar
SFR	Swiss franc
YEN	Japanese yen
CAD	Canadian dollar
ÖS	Austrian schilling

Other abbreviations

ACP	African, Caribbean and Pacific countries having signed the Lomé Convention
ECSC	European Coal and Steel Community
EDF	European Development Fund
EIB	European Investment Bank
EMCF	European Monetary Cooperation Fund
EMS	European Monetary System
ERDF	European Regional Development Fund
Euratom	European Atomic Energy Community
Eurostat	Statistical Office of the European Communities (SOEC)
GDP (GNP)	Gross domestic (national) product
GFCF	Gross fixed capital formation
LDCs	Less-developed countries
Mio	Million
Mrd	1 000 million
NCI	New Community Instrument
OCTs	Overseas countries and territories
OECD	Organization for Economic Cooperation and Development
OPEC	Organization of Petroleum Exporting Countries
PPS	Purchasing power standard
SMEs	Small and medium-sized enterprises
toe	Tonne of oil equivalent
:	Not available

iv

Contents

Tables

Graphs

Chapter 1

Overview: main policy issues

1.0. Introduction

The Danish economy has been characterized by a disappointing rate of growth in recent years compared to the rest of the Community (see Graph 1). GDP growth was only around 1% on average per year in the period 1987-92 and the unemployment rate has gradually increased to a current level of 12,4% (August 1993, national definition). Reversal of this upward trend in unemployment is the biggest challenge in the Danish economy, and faster growth will be necessary to achieve this.

Slow growth, in a period when the rest of the Community saw high growth rates, was due to an adjustment of the Danish economy after the boom between 1983 and 1986. The boom had caused a deterioration of nominal fundamentals and necessitated a tightening of policies in 1986-87 (see below and country study on Denmark from April 1991). At the beginning of 1992, Danish macroeconomic fundamentals had strengthened and were among the best in the Community. The current account showed a record high surplus of 3% of GDP in 1992 after more than 25 years of deficits. In 1992, inflation was down to 2,1% and the public deficit was moderate (2,5% of GDP). The adjustment process was seemingly coming to an end. The problem of high unemployment remained, but the stage was set for a return to higher growth.

The Danish krone appreciated about 7,2% in effective terms from the first half of 1992 to March 1993, mainly due to the devaluation of other currencies. The deterioration in Danish cost competitiveness, together with the recession in Sweden and Germany, threatened Danish exports at least in the short run. Export growth slowed in the second half of 1992 and declined at the beginning of 1993. Since the widening of the ERM bands, the nominal effective exchange rate has depreciated, but remains approximately 2% above its June 1992 level. Moderate wage increases should again contribute to an improvement in Danish competitiveness. However, continued improvement in Danish competitiveness will be difficult without further structural adjustment.

In principle, the integrating European economy provides many opportunities for Denmark and should enable the Danish economy to enjoy a period of higher economic growth, if the necessary adjustments in Danish supply conditions are made. However, the currency developments since September 1992 and the weak international economy have complicated the situation by reducing short-term prospects for higher growth and lower unemployment. The possibilities of using general economic policies to boost the economy in the short term are constrained. Monetary policy is oriented towards exchange-rate stability. First modest fiscal expansionary measures were undertaken in 1992 and 1993.

In May 1993 a discretionary fiscal package including a tax reform, a labour-market reform as well as additional measures to support industrial development and construction was presented and will be taking effect from 1 January 1994. The package aims at boosting private sector confidence and achieving structural improvements. First calculations indicate that the package provides a direct fiscal expansion of about 1,5% of GDP and will boost GDP growth by 1,8% in 1994. Given the quantitative importance, the programme implies a change in both the trend of fiscal deficits as well as a more direct assignment of fiscal policy towards cyclical stabilization. The success of the package in the short term will very much depend on the turn-around it may induce in private sector confidence. In the medium to long term, growth and employment prospects seem to be quite good with the present stability-oriented macroeconomic framework.

This study discusses the medium- to long-term supply-side issues facing Denmark in the integrating European economy as well as the risks arising from the developments since September 1992. The first section provides an overview of the macroeconomic developments in the 1982-92 period, analyses in a general way the structural improvements in the supply conditions achieved, and discusses the implications of the ERM turmoil.

In Section 2, the nature of Danish unemployment and structural problems on the Danish labour market are discussed. It is concluded that, while major structural problems prevent unemployment from falling below 8%, demographic trends also necessitate a somewhat different emphasis in labour-market policies. Labour-market reforms will have to be part of any growth strategy.

In Section 3, public finances and particularly taxation issues are discussed. It is argued that structural problems remain in the tax system. These problems have supply-side consequences and are related to the labour-market issues; but the large public sector in itself limits the options for structural change in taxation.

1

Section 4 discusses the prospects for job creation through industrial development. It is concluded that, at least in the medium term, Danish industry is in a good position in the integrating European economy, but the prospects for employment creation are mixed. Furthermore, the analysis presented in Section 5 on the developments of the financial sector, which has undergone particularly big changes in recent years, points to a similar downbeat employment outlook for this sector. The main conclusions of the study are presented in Section 6.

1.1. Macroeconomic developments 1982-92

1.1.1. 1982-87: Improved confidence and high growth

In 1982 the Danish Government decided to introduce a tight fiscal policy and pursue a hard currency stance. Furthermore, supply-side measures with the aim of greater labour-market flexibility, particularly the suspension and later abolition of the wage indexation scheme, were implemented. Inflation subsequently dropped from more than 10% in 1982 to 3,5% in 1985 and interest rates declined. Demand expectations improved, leading to higher investment and consumer spending. In the four years to 1986, output rose 16%. The boom in output was driven entirely by domestic demand.

The development in expectations is a key element in understanding the evolution of the Danish economy in the 1980s. As seen from Graph 2, consumer confidence rose markedly in 1982-83 and remained high throughout the boom period 1983-86 following the change in policies. The government clearly stated that the primary aim of monetary policy was price stability, which was thought to be best served by adopting a binding exchange-rate commitment as provided by the ERM. Although labour cost pressures accelerated in the later phase of the boom period, price expectations were stabilized by the steep fall in commodity prices.

However, in 1986 the current-account deficit had deteriorated to 5,5% of GDP following the surge in domestic demand. This was clearly unsustainable in view of the relatively large external debt accumulated over the preceding 20 years and more. Unemployment decreased from 10,5% in 1983 to 8% in 1986. At this level of unemployment, bottlenecks developed in the labour market; these resulted in very high wage increases in the 1987 wage settlement, suggesting that the NAIRU was then about 8% and that structural problems persist on the labour market. Nominal unit labour

costs increased by more than 8% in 1987, fuelling inflationary pressures. The constraint on monetary policy, as a result of the ERM commitment, did not allow a sufficient tightening of monetary policy in the early phase of the boom despite fiscal contraction.

By 1986, the deterioration in the current account, the prospects of higher inflation and a worsening of competitiveness led the government to introduce an austerity programme in order to contain private consumption. In the spring of 1986, excise duties on energy were increased substantially, and in the autumn a surcharge on interest payments on consumer credits was introduced. Furthermore, in the 1987 tax reform the marginal tax rate on net capital income was reduced to 50% implying a further reduction in the tax relief for interest payments. This also contributed to the decline of house prices in the following years. These measures brought the growth period to a halt, and marked the beginning of the long 1987-92 period of slow growth.

1.1.2. 1987 to September 1992: slow growth, but stronger nominal fundamentals

The austerity programme, introduced at the peak of the cycle in 1986, had a significant influence on expectations (see Graph 2). Expectations of lower demand, due to tight fiscal policy measures and deteriorating competitiveness, in turn had a strong impact on confidence. Investors feared that their investments, based on previous optimistic expectations, could become unprofitable. Thus, new investments were substantially cut back or postponed. Private consumption declined in 1987-88 and private households' savings increased. All in all, the 1987-92 period was characterized by weak domestic demand, resulting in stagnant GDP growth. On average, growth did not exceed 1% per year in this period, which was not large enough to prevent unemployment from rising, since the labour force and productivity also increased over the period.

On the external side, the main policy strategy since 1987 consisted of regaining cost competitiveness, which had deteriorated in the boom years. The hard currency stance was not questioned, implying that competitiveness had to be gained through moderate increases in unit labour costs relative to main trading partners. The strategy proved successful as competitiveness improved about 9% and market shares were gained between 1987 and mid-1992. The improvement in competitiveness, combined with a favourable economic growth in the main partner countries and special factors, notably German unification and increased Danish production of North Sea oil and gas, led to a strong export performance, which was the main source of growth in the

GRAPH 1: **GDP growth rates: Denmark and EUR 12**

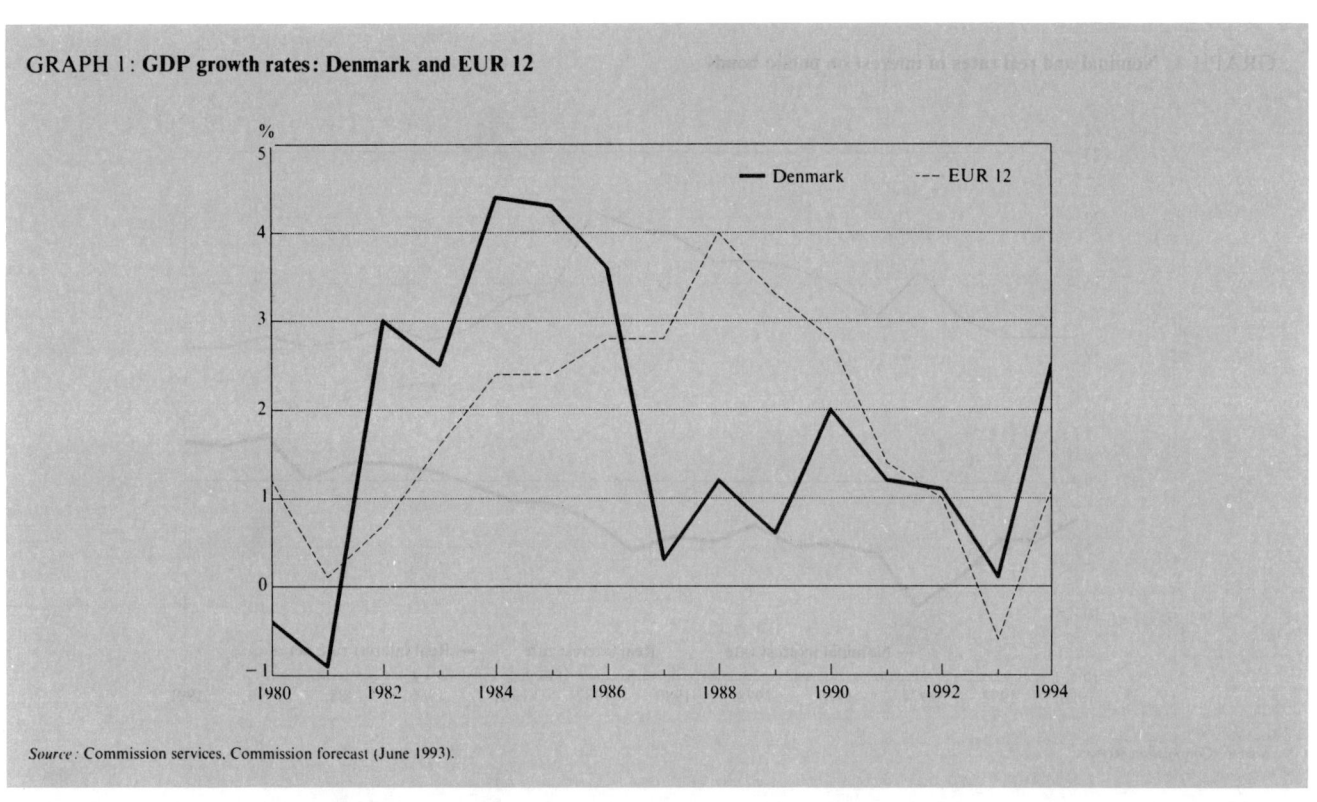

Source: Commission services. Commission forecast (June 1993).

GRAPH 2: **Consumer confidence indicator**

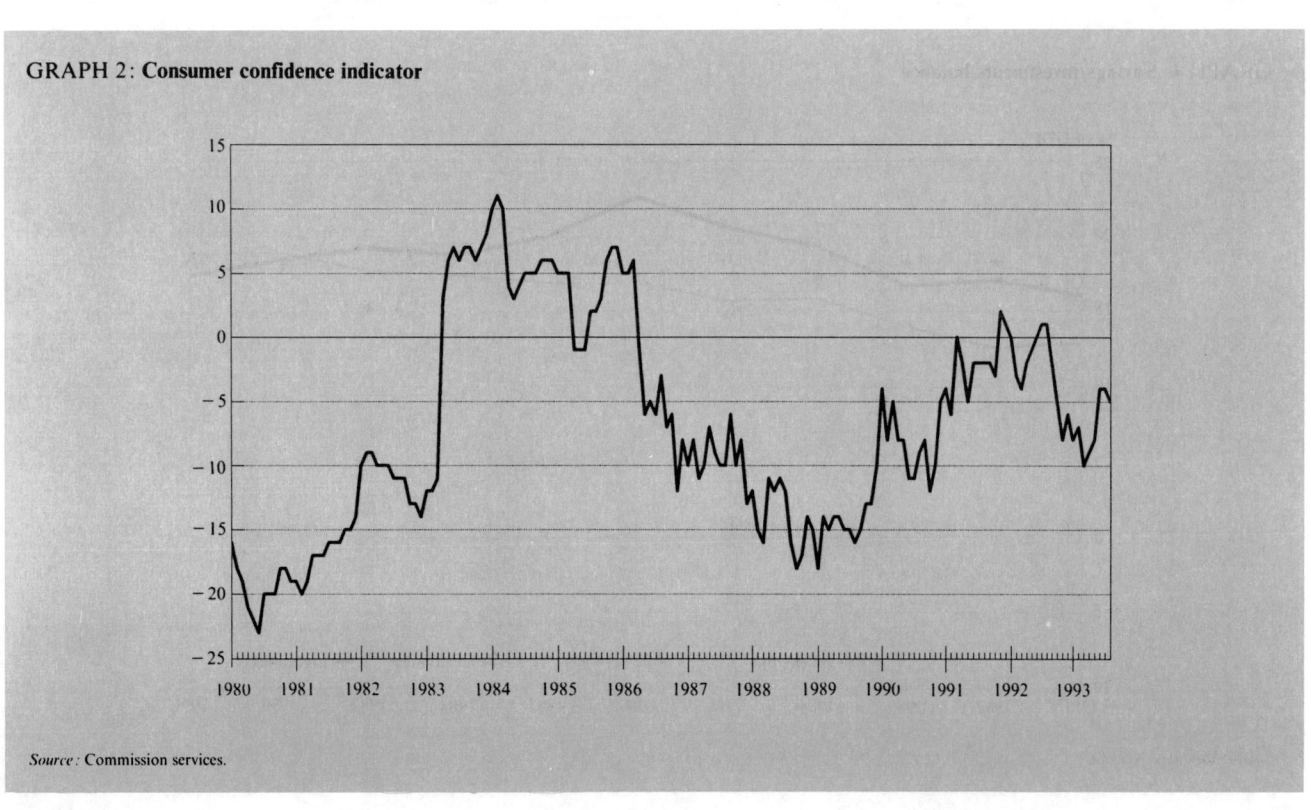

Source: Commission services.

GRAPH 3: **Nominal and real rates of interest on public bonds**

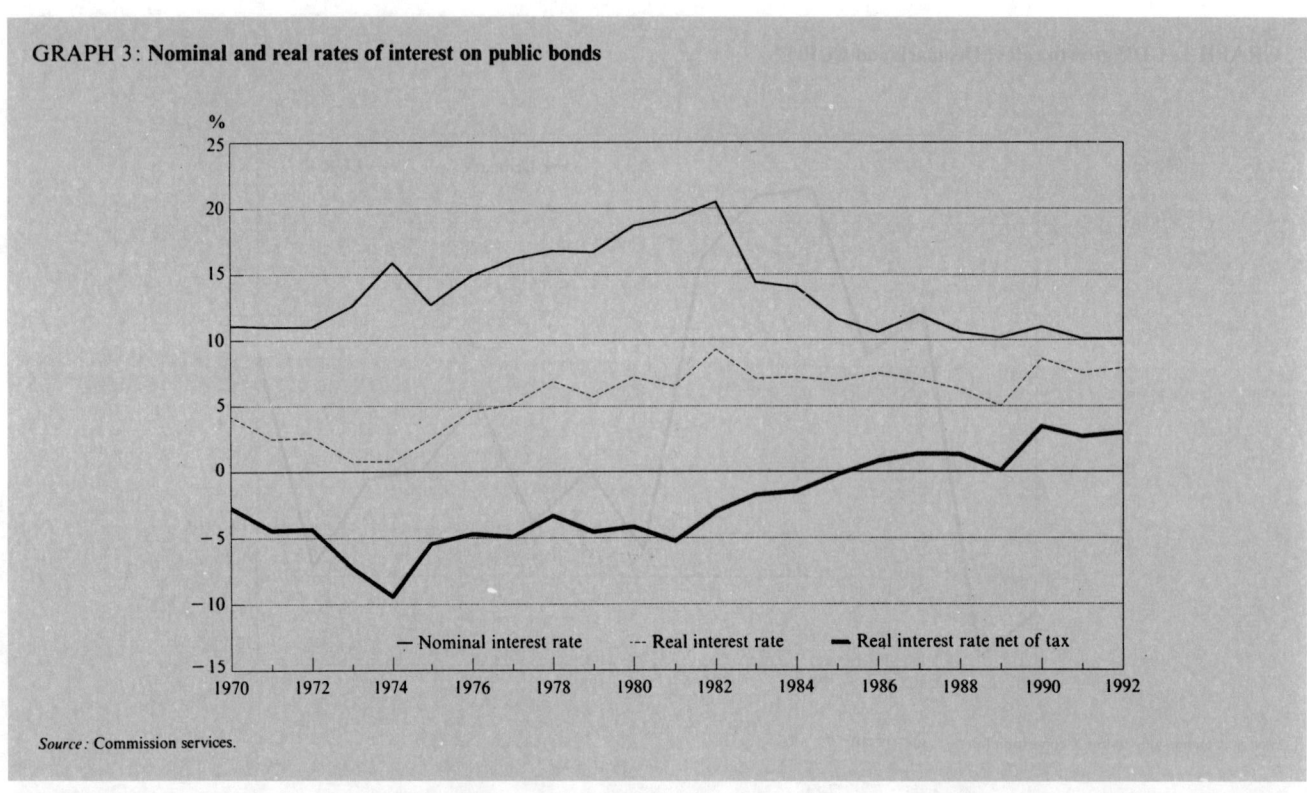

Source: Commission services.

GRAPH 4: **Savings/investments balance**

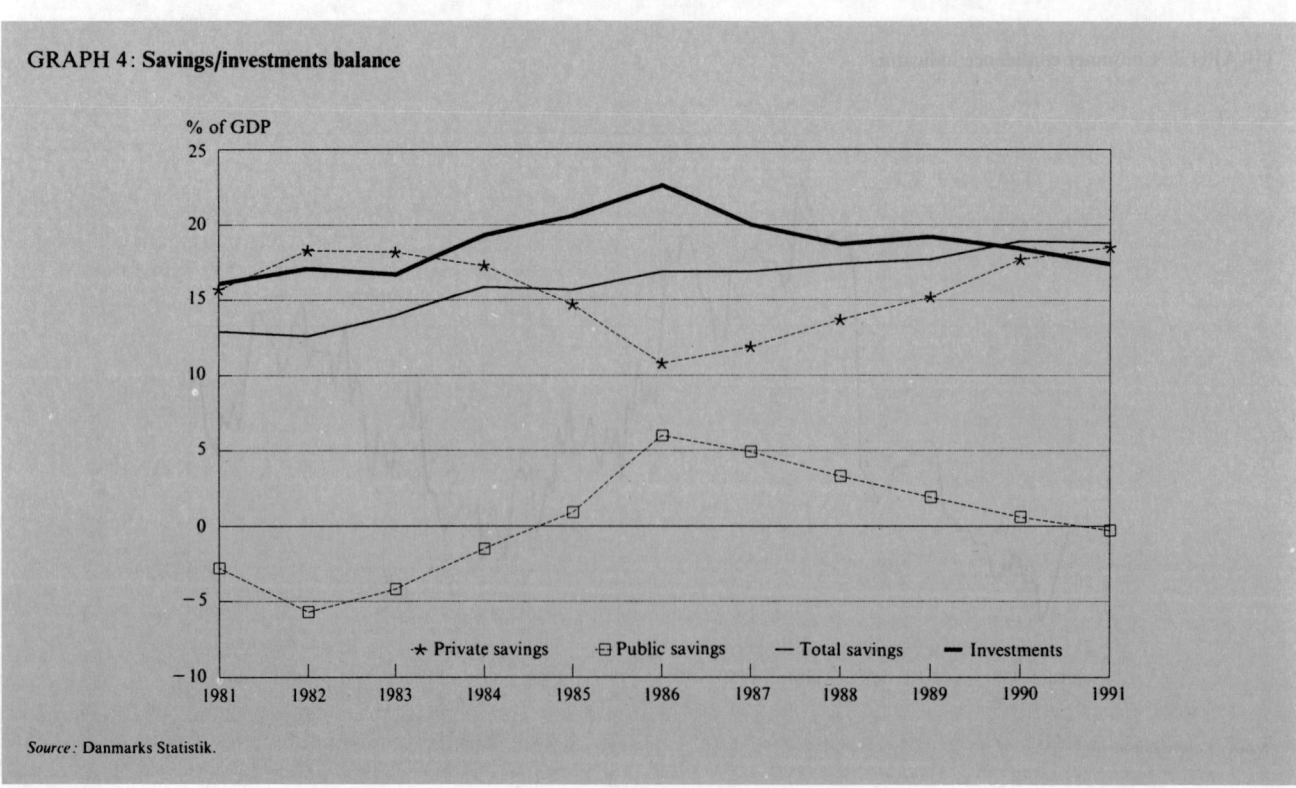

Source: Danmarks Statistik.

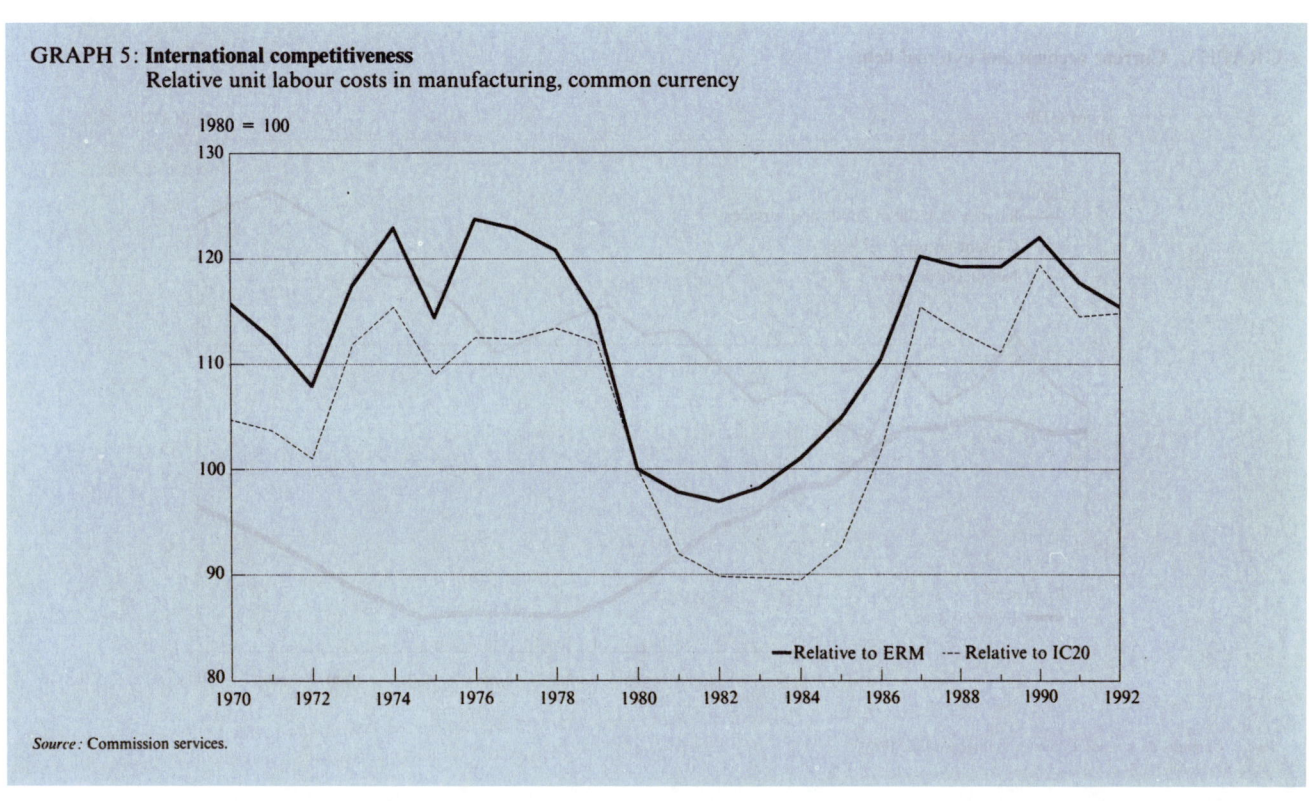

GRAPH 5: **International competitiveness**
Relative unit labour costs in manufacturing, common currency

1980 = 100

—Relative to ERM --- Relative to IC20

Source: Commission services.

1987-92 period. At the same time, domestic demand was weak and private savings high. The current account gradually improved, and for the first time in more than 25 years showed a surplus in 1990, allowing Denmark to begin reducing its large external debt.

The hard currency stance, the moderate wage increases, and weak internal demand over the period led to a significant reduction in inflation. Consumer price inflation fell from 7,7% in 1986 to 2,1% in 1992, which was the lowest in the Community. However, low growth and the increase in unemployment contributed to a deterioration in public finances. In 1986, the public finances were in a surplus of 3,4% in terms of GDP; despite the 1986-87 austerity measures, this gradually deteriorated to a deficit of 2,5% in 1992.

All in all, nominal macroeconomic fundamentals improved considerably in the period 1987 to September 1992: inflation was brought under control, the current account moved into a healthy surplus allowing Denmark to reduce its foreign debt while the deteriorating trend in public finances was kept under control; however, growth remained disappointing and unemployment increased. In this respect, as will be discussed in the next section, the improvement in nominal fundamentals does not simply reflect trade-offs between unemployment, inflation, and the current account, but an improvement in the underlying supply conditions as well.

1.1.3. Improvements in supply conditions in the 1980s

An improvement in supply conditions enables an economy to simultaneously reduce imbalances. This can for example involve structural adjustments which change the behaviour of economic agents through institutional reforms or by bringing about a change in the macroeconomic policy regime. External developments like factor price developments or the opening of formerly closed markets may also improve supply conditions.

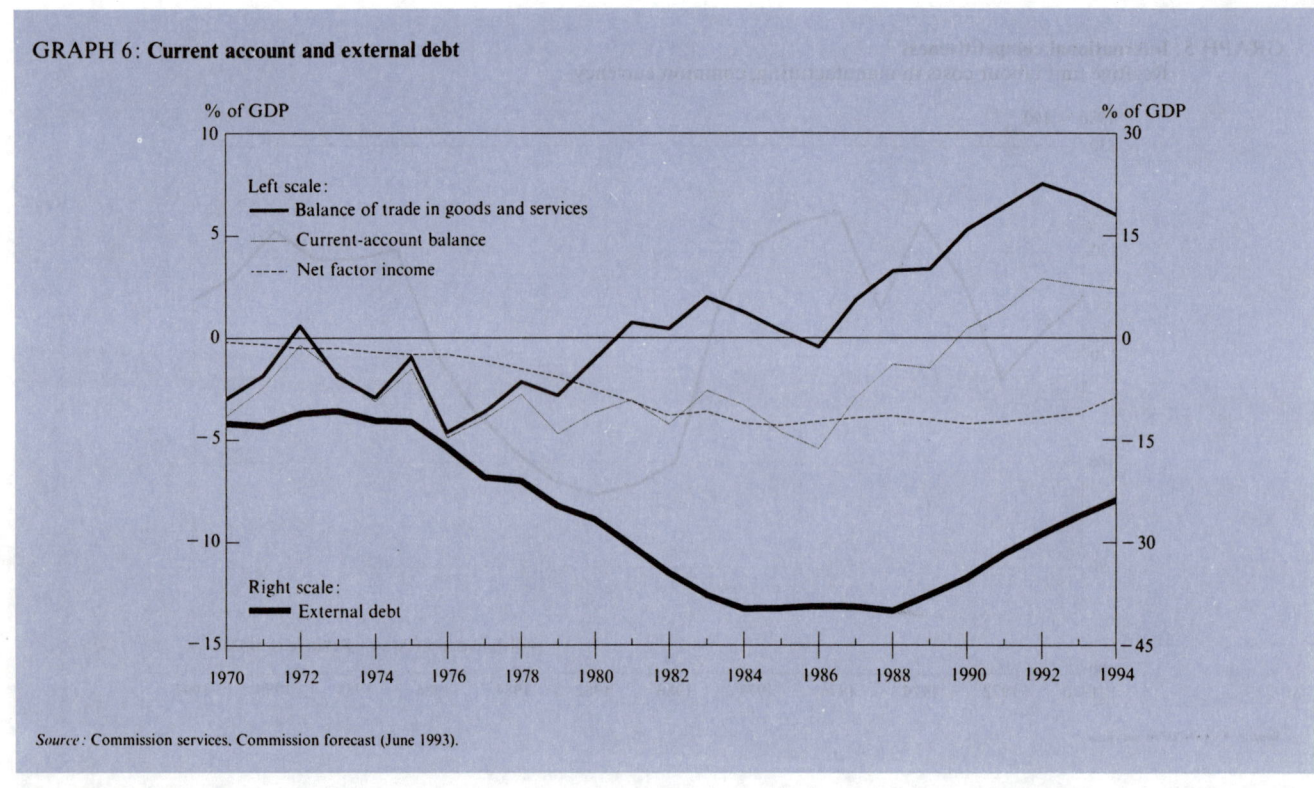

GRAPH 6: **Current account and external debt**

% of GDP

Left scale:
— Balance of trade in goods and services
— Current-account balance
----- Net factor income

Right scale:
— External debt

Source: Commission services. Commission forecast (June 1993).

It is difficult to quantify or to test for structural improvements. However, it is possible to assess, on an aggregate level, the direction of changes by looking simultaneously at the inflation/unemployment and unemployment/current-account balances.

In an inflation/unemployment diagram, short-term movements would be expected to follow a normal negatively sloped Phillips curve. An anti-inflationary strategy could thus initially lead to higher unemployment. However, in the long term, as economic agents change their behaviour, a shift in the short-term trade-off would occur. Long-term structural improvements would, therefore, be expected to result in shifts in the short-term Phillips curve towards the origin, thus leading to a simultaneous reduction in imbalances.

Indications of shifts in the short-term Phillips curve can be obtained by examining movements in the inflation/unemployment balance over a longer period of time. In Graph 7, the direction of the shift between 1981-82 and 1991-92 is shown. Belgium and the Netherlands appear to have achieved structural improvements, whereas the situation for

(West) Germany was largely unchanged. Judging from Graph 7, it is doubtful whether France, the United Kingdom, and Italy have achieved structural improvements with respect to the inflation/unemployment trade-off. However, comparing only two observation points might not tell the whole story.

A three-year moving average of the inflation/unemployment relationship is shown for Denmark, as the focus of this study is on Denmark. The graph tends to show an improving relationship until 1987. Inflation was reduced by wage moderation and, when wages started to increase in 1986, by rapidly falling commodity prices. At the same time the unemployment rate was reduced by 2 percentage points. A main element of structural improvement has been, among other things, the abolition of the wage indexation scheme.

However, confidence in supply-side improvements seems to have been interrupted in the aftermath of the 1987 wage slippage. The austerity measures in 1986-87 (including the 1987 tax reform) depressed domestic demand by increasing the incentive to save, and unemployment started rising in 1987. It can be said that the chosen hard currency option accelerated the process of disinflation, but it took until 1992 before improving competitiveness seemed to have brought to a halt the process of increasing unemployment. Indeed 1992 could have marked a turning point in the relationship, if the appreciation of the krone together with a loss in confidence had not caused significantly deteriorating growth prospects.

An improvement in supply-side conditions strengthens private sector confidence and stimulates private sector expectations. Therefore, a supply-side improvement would initially be associated with lower unemployment, but the current account would probably deteriorate. Over time, if better supply-side conditions improve competitiveness through strong investment, a low rate of unemployment would be achievable with an improved current-account balance.

As seen from Graph 8, the Netherlands and Belgium have apparently achieved structural improvements on the current-account/unemployment trade-off, while the situation for (West) Germany is by and large unchanged. France and Italy have probably not seen any structural improvements,

whereas the conditions in the UK have seemingly worsened, which could also be due partly to lower oil prices.

Again, the story on Denmark is twofold. Increased private sector spending due to improved private sector confidence led to a significant decline in unemployment and a deterioration of the current account until 1986. Starting in 1987, due to the austerity measures, the current-account balance improved dramatically, mainly a reflection of weak domestic demand, but also as time went on, improving competitiveness. Again, 1992 may have marked a turning point: improved competitiveness was beginning to influence private sector confidence positively which could have spurred the possibility of a reduction in unemployment. It should, however, be noted that special developments, like the impact of German unification and rising oil and gas production, were important determinants of the current-account improvement as well.

All in all, it can be concluded that the improvements in nominal fundamentals partly reflect the implementation of supply-side reforms; but important structural problems remain, for example, in the labour market and in the tax structure.

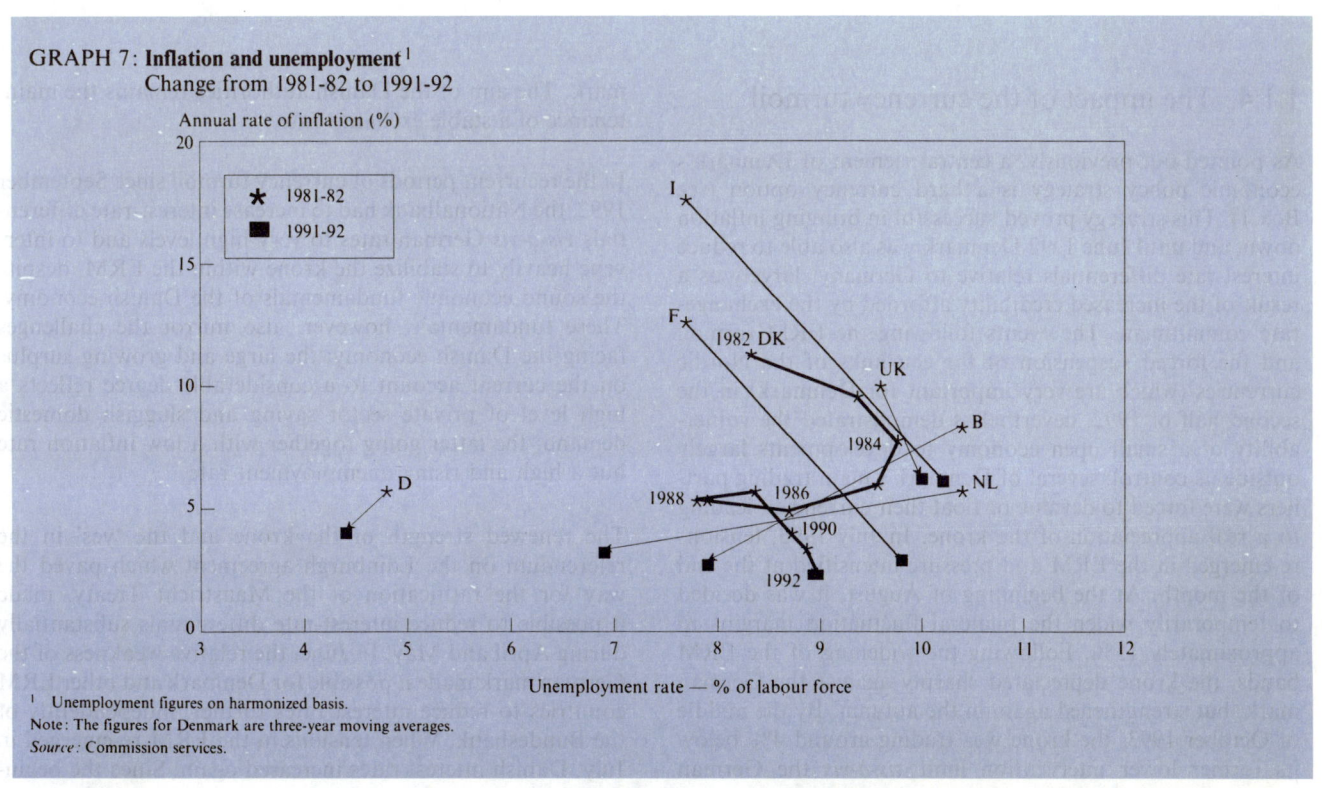

GRAPH 7: **Inflation and unemployment** [1]
Change from 1981-82 to 1991-92

Annual rate of inflation (%)

* 1981-82
■ 1991-92

Unemployment rate — % of labour force

[1] Unemployment figures on harmonized basis.
Note: The figures for Denmark are three-year moving averages.
Source: Commission services.

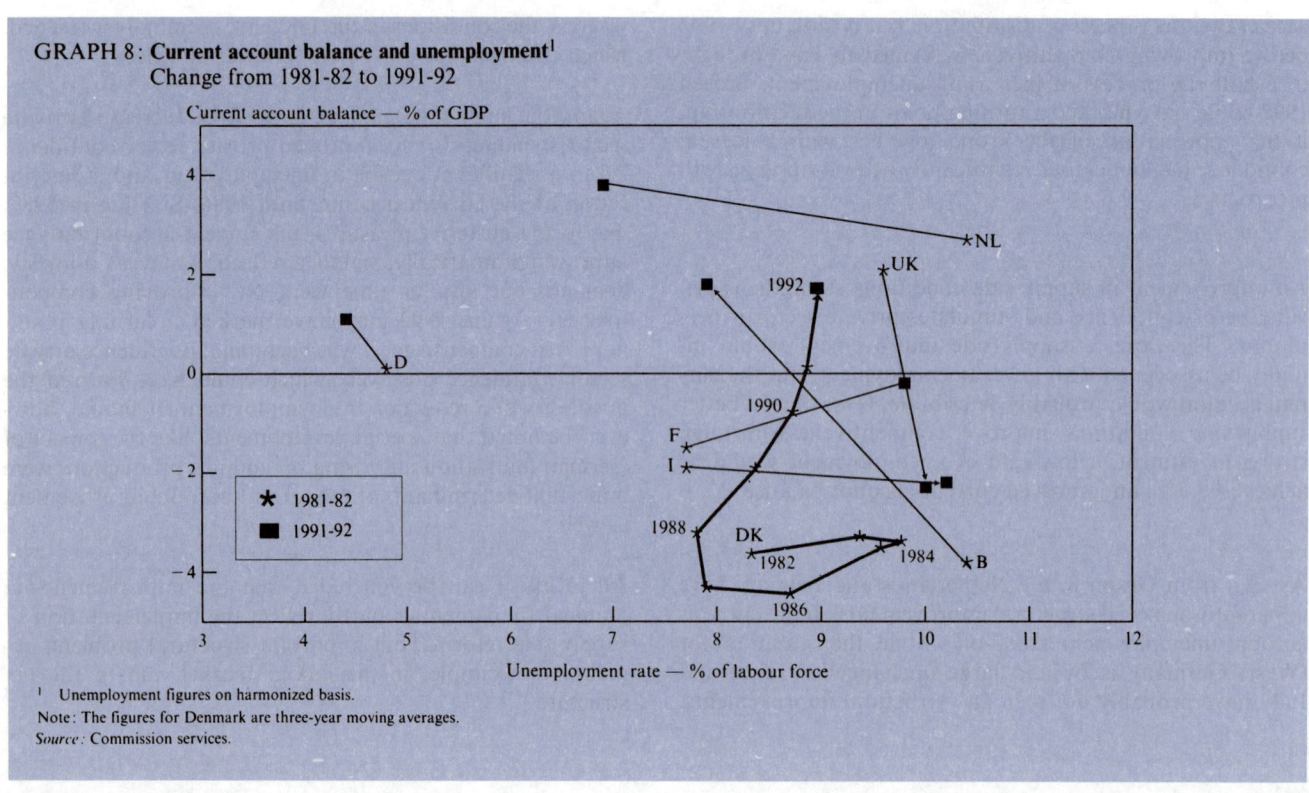

GRAPH 8: **Current account balance and unemployment**[1]
Change from 1981-82 to 1991-92

Current account balance — % of GDP

Legend:
★ 1981-82
■ 1991-92

Unemployment rate — % of labour force

[1] Unemployment figures on harmonized basis.
Note: The figures for Denmark are three-year moving averages.
Source: Commission services.

1.1.4. The impact of the currency turmoil

As pointed out previously, a central element of Denmark's economic policy strategy is a hard currency option (see Box 1). This strategy proved successful in bringing inflation down, and until June 1992 Denmark was also able to reduce interest-rate differentials relative to Germany, largely as a result of the increased credibility afforded by the exchange-rate commitment. The events following the ERM turmoil and the forced suspension of the ecu links of the Nordic currencies (which are very important for Denmark) in the second half of 1992, nevertheless demonstrated the vulnerability of a small open economy to developments largely outside its control: several of Denmark's main trading partners were forced to devalue or float their currencies, leading to a real appreciation of the krone. In July 1993, tensions re-emerged in the ERM and pressure intensified at the end of the month. At the beginning of August, it was decided to temporarily widen the bilateral fluctuation margins to approximately 15%. Following the widening of the ERM bands, the krone depreciated sharply against the German mark, but strengthened again in the autumn. By the middle of October 1993, the krone was trading around 4% below its former lower intervention limit *vis-à-vis* the German

mark. The aim of the Danish authorities remains the maintenance of a stable exchange rate.

In the recurrent periods of currency turmoil since September 1992, the Nationalbank had to increase interest-rate differentials *vis-à-vis* German rates to very high levels and to intervene heavily to stabilize the krone within the ERM, despite the sound economic fundamentals of the Danish economy. These fundamentals, however, also mirror the challenges facing the Danish economy: the large and growing surplus on the current account to a considerable degree reflects a high level of private sector saving and sluggish domestic demand; the latter going together with a low inflation rate but a high and rising unemployment rate.

The renewed strength of the krone and the 'yes' in the referendum on the Edinburgh agreement which paved the way for the ratification of the Maastricht Treaty, made it possible to reduce interest-rate differentials substantially during April and May. In June, the relative weakness of the German mark made it possible for Denmark and other ERM countries to reduce interest rates further, independently of the Bundesbank. When tensions in the ERM re-emerged in July, Danish interest rates increased again. Since the beginning of August, interest rates have, however, been gradually lowered, but the short-term interest-rate differential with Germany remained relatively high at 2,25% in mid-October.

After 10 years experience of hard currency option, which has been beneficial in several respects, Denmark is now facing a situation of high real interest rates. As seen in Graph 10, real interest rates increased substantially in 1992-93, and remain high in the light of the economic situation. Nominal interest rates may fall further, but real interest rates are likely to remain higher than elsewhere.

The direct effect of the pressure on the krone, via a feed-through of higher money-market rates to lending rates, has been less in Denmark than in many other countries, as a relatively large proportion of private sector borrowing is in the form of fixed-rate mortgage loans. The ERM turmoil and the high level of real interest rates have, however, contributed to the current low level of consumer confidence. Given their high level of debt, Danish households may choose to reduce or stabilize their debt level rather than increase spending. The high level of real interest rates will

also discourage investment in real assets relative to financial assets.

The loss of competitiveness as result of the ERM turmoil initially reversed the earlier gains from competitive disinflation and implied a setback for the exporting and import-competing industries. On the other hand, Denmark has regained some competitiveness through the moderate devaluation following the widening of the ERM band. Furthermore, wage moderation is likely to continue, which will ease domestically generated inflationary pressure, and the policy of stabilizing the krone should ensure modest imported inflation. In the longer run, higher inflation than would otherwise have been the case in countries which have devalued substantially or whose currencies have depreciated sharply after floating should help Denmark to improve its competitiveness. However, the scope for improving competitiveness by maintaining lower domestic inflation than partner countries may be limited. Firstly, in the present high unemployment and low growth environment, such a policy may prove too costly. In 1987, when Denmark started this process, the unemployment rate was 8% (national definition) and the inflation rate 4,9%, compared to a current 12,4% (August 1993) and 1,5% (September 1993) respectively. Sec-

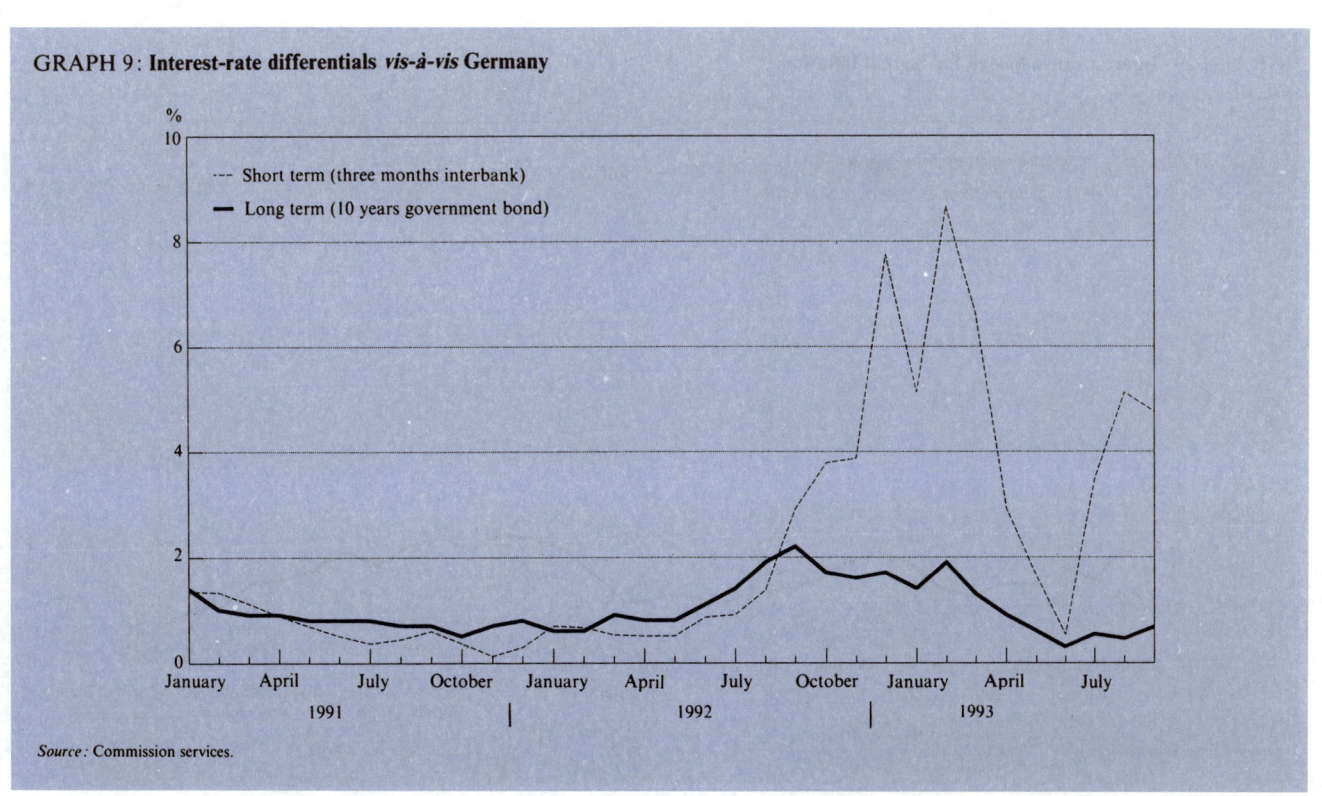

GRAPH 9: Interest-rate differentials *vis-à-vis* Germany

--- Short term (three months interbank)
— Long term (10 years government bond)

Source: Commission services.

ondly, Denmark, along with other narrow-band countries in the ERM, gained competitiveness as a result of the rise in German inflation after unification. A fall in the German inflation rate towards the Bundesbank target of 2%, would make it much more difficult for Denmark to improve bilateral competitiveness further. However, given the present cost level *vis-à-vis* Germany, developments among Denmark's other trading partners, particularly those that have had to devalue substantially, will be more critical from a Danish point of view. In addition, the Danish economy will benefit if lower German inflation leads to a reduction of interest rates in Germany and subsequently in Denmark.

1.1.5. High unemployment remains the biggest challenge

In face of high and increasing unemployment, it was decided to provide a fiscal stimulus to the economy in 1993. The budget for 1993 included various measures, among others increased expenditure on education, a support fund for entrepreneurs, support for maintenance and repairs of housing and an acceleration of planned public investment. The new government, which came into power in January 1993, has launched a major fiscal package including tax reform, labour-market reform, and additional measures to support industrial development and construction. The package, which will take effect from 1 January 1994, should contribute to a decline in unemployment.

In the medium to long term, structural improvements are necessary in order to achieve a sustainable reduction in unemployment. Supply conditions improved in the 1980s, but further improvements will be necessary in order to benefit fully from the internal market and to reduce unemployment. A credible commitment to pursue supply-side improvements will not only increase medium-term growth prospects but would also trigger favourable effects on expectations in the short term. The recent fiscal package also aims at structural improvements in the tax system and the labour market, and in many ways points in the right direction, as is discussed in the following sections.

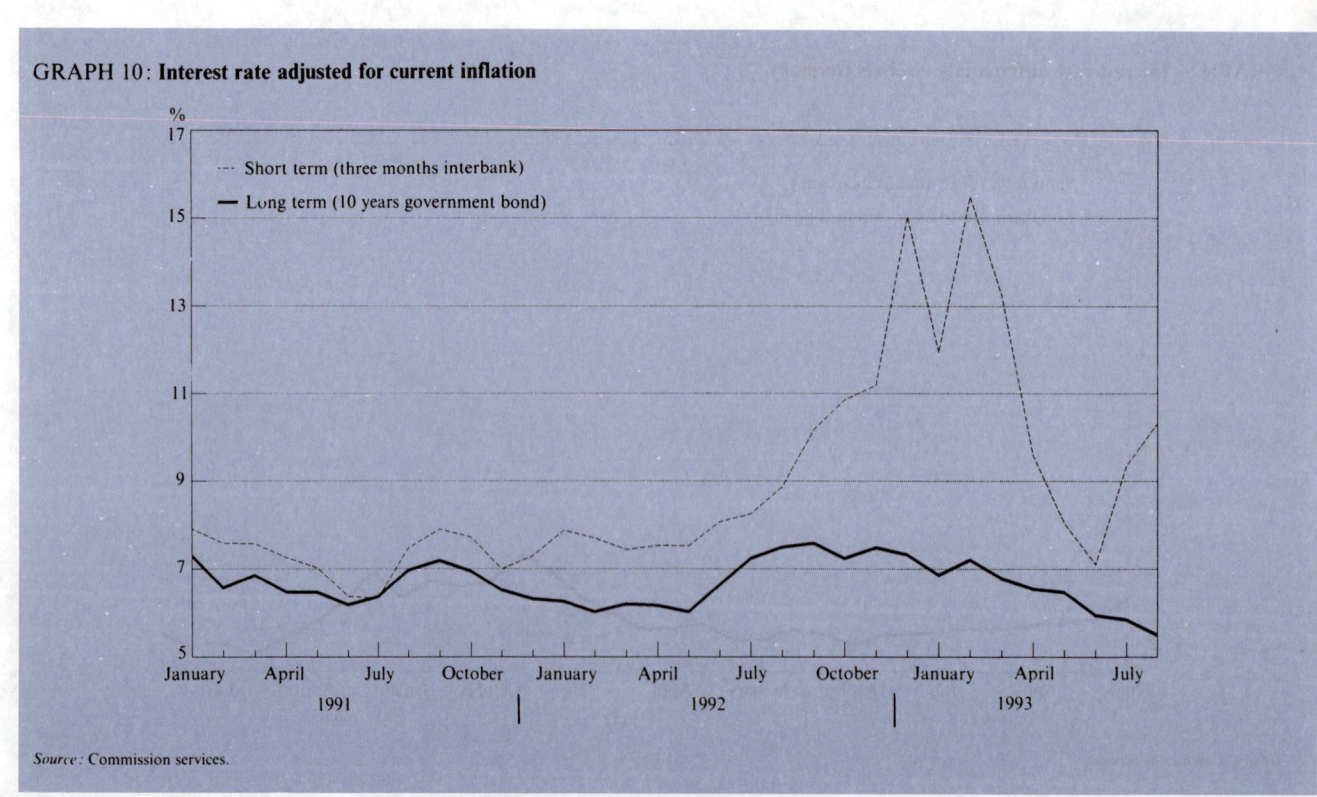

GRAPH 10: **Interest rate adjusted for current inflation**

Source: Commission services.

1.2. Unemployment and the Danish labour market

1.2.1. The nature of Danish unemployment

The average unemployment rate was 11,4%[1] in 1992. It is on a rising trend, and reached 12,4% in August 1993. Moreover, people in early retirement and various job-creation schemes amount to about 4% of the labour force. Spending on active and passive labour-market measures was close to 8% of GDP in 1992.

The high unemployment rate of the 1980s was not caused by a deterioration in employment creation; while the employment level has declined since 1987, it remains at a higher level than in 1980. The main reason for the increase in

unemployment in the 1980s has been the escalating structural problems in the labour market, but a relatively high number of youngsters entering the labour force, and a higher activity rate of women have also contributed substantially to the increase. The number of youngsters entering the labour force is decreasing, and the labour force is even likely to contract from the mid-1990s onwards. However, this will not necessarily solve the unemployment problem, which is to a large extent structural. Furthermore, the ageing of the labour force will pose new challenges.

The evidence from the 1986 boom year, where bottlenecks developed in the labour market and excessive wage increases resulted, suggest — as a rough estimate — that the minimum attainable rate of unemployment which does not lead to higher inflationary pressures (the NAIRU), was then as high as 8%. The part of unemployment, which is due to the business cycle, was accordingly at most 4 percentage points of the total unemployment rate. Consequently, the Danish labour market would seem to be able to accommodate a moderate recovery without endangering stability, but a more substantial reduction would require reducing the structural problems on the labour market. However, the longer the cyclical component of unemployment persists, the greater the

---

[1] National definition, which is higher than the international definition by about 1,5 percentage points. A main reason for the difference is the treatment of short unemployment periods. The Danish labour market is characterized by a high number of short unemployment periods, which are included in the national, but not the international definition of unemployment.

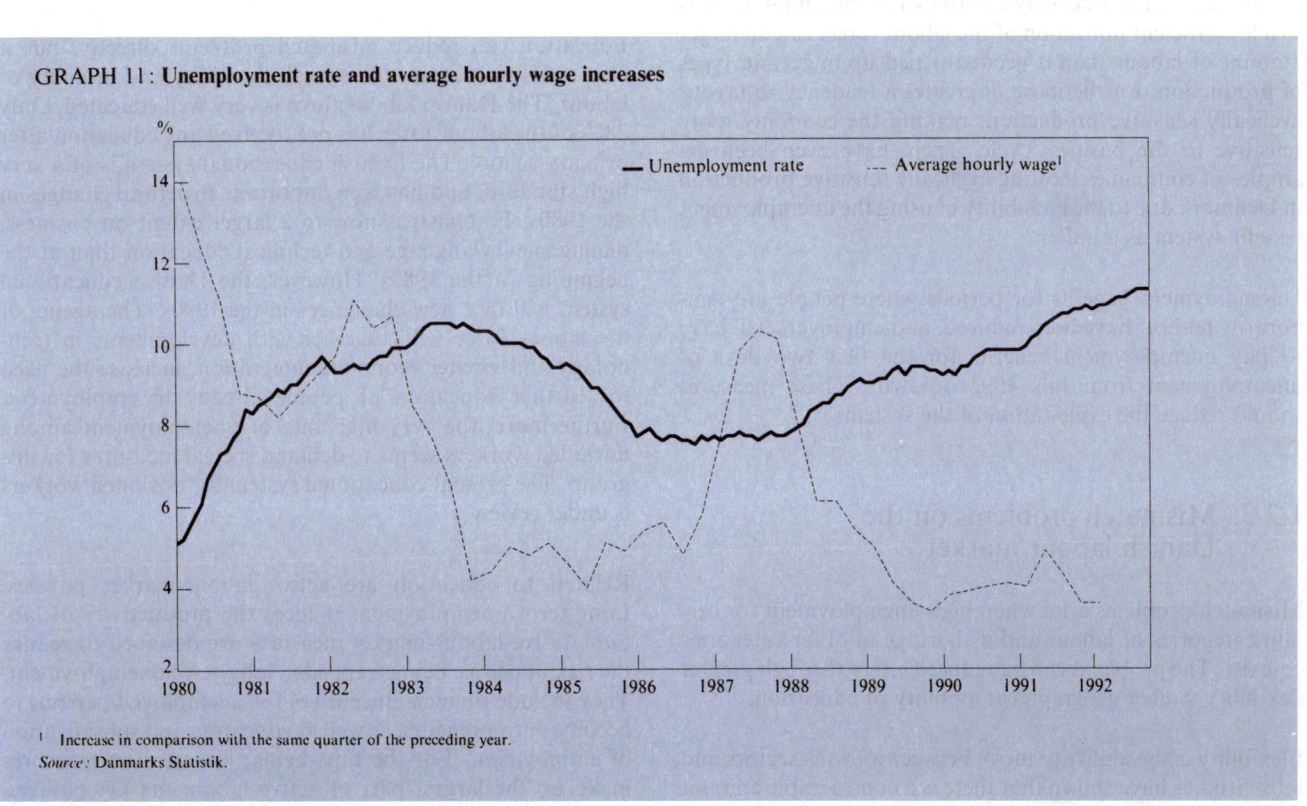

GRAPH 11: **Unemployment rate and average hourly wage increases**

— Unemployment rate   --- Average hourly wage[1]

[1] Increase in comparison with the same quarter of the preceding year.
Source: Danmarks Statistik.

hysteresis in the unemployment rate becomes. The structural problems are in particular due to a high number of temporary layoffs, mismatch problems and insufficient wage flexibility.

1.2.2. The problem of temporary layoffs

Short-term unemployment is a particular characteristic of the Danish labour market. An expert committee appointed by the Danish Government estimated that short-term unemployment contributes 0,5 of a percentage point to total unemployment, but this is probably an underestimate. The main reason for the high number of temporary layoffs is the combination of a generous unemployment benefit system and limited restrictions on employers in shedding unwanted labour. The liberal firing rules contribute to higher flexibility on the labour market and are as such beneficial. However, the relatively easy access to generous unemployment benefits has enabled some sectors like the harbours and the fishing industry to use the unemployment benefit system as a buffer, laying people off in periods of low demand.

The problem with the large number of temporary layoffs is not simply significant additional expenditure on unemployment benefits. To the extent that the current system gives employers greater flexibility in production planning, it leads to a less efficient utilization of the labour force, since a larger amount of labour than is needed is tied up in certain types of production. Furthermore, it creates a tendency to favour cyclically sensitive production, making the economy more sensitive to the business cycle. There have even been examples of companies locating cyclically sensitive production in Denmark due to the possibility of using the unemployment benefit system as a buffer.

Unemployment benefits for periods where people are temporarily laid off have been reduced, and employers will have to pay unemployment benefits for the first two days of unemployment from July 1993 onwards. These measures should reduce the exploitation of the system.

1.2.3. Mismatch problems on the Danish labour market

Mismatch problems arise when high unemployment for certain categories of labour and a shortage in other categories co-exist. The problems can be reduced either through greater flexibility, higher geographical mobility or education.

Flexibility is the ability to move between various sectors and jobs. Studies have shown that there is a considerable amount of potential flexibility between related educational groups and sectors. However, there are still some barriers to flexibility. Firstly, it is hampered by the structure of industrial relations. The trade unions are still organized in a traditional structure, which can result in sub-optimal organization of labour. A structure like in Sweden or Germany, where all employees of a firm are organized in one union would seem more appropriate. Furthermore, the generous unemployment benefit system makes flexibility less attractive. The problem is aggravated by a limited scope for the authorities to force the unemployed to accept jobs, thus increasing the risk of the unemployed being stuck in long-term unemployment.

Geographical mobility seems to be too low. Only a small percentage of job changes also involve a geographical move. The increased number of double-income families and the difficulty of selling old accommodation before new is acquired — due to the slump in the housing market — have reduced geographical mobility. Furthermore, it is difficult to find moderately priced rental accommodation. Over the years, improvements to the infrastructure have reduced the need for a physical move in connection with a change of job. However, regional differences exist in unemployment rates — in Denmark as elsewhere — indicating a need for higher geographical mobility.

Education can reduce mismatch problems directly, but it also tends to increase the overall flexibility and mobility of labour. The Danish labour force is very well educated. Only 28% of the labour force has not received any education after primary school. The Danish educational system is of a very high standard, and has seen important structural changes in the 1980s. Emphasis is now to a larger extent on business, management, language and technical education than at the beginning of the 1980s. However, the Danish educational system will face new challenges in the 1990s. The ageing of the labour force will, together with developments in technology and greater economic integration, increase the need for further education of people already in employment. Furthermore, the very high rate of unemployment among unskilled workers seems to demand special measures for this group. The present educational system for unskilled workers is under review.

Related to education are active labour-market policies. Long-term unemployment reduces the productivity of labour. Active labour-market measures are designed to reduce the risk of people being trapped in long-term unemployment. They include financial incentives for unemployed persons to become entrepreneurs, as well as education and subsidization of employment. For the time being, job-creation measures make up the largest part of active labour-market policies.

However, a high NAIRU indicates that the resources may not be utilized as effectively as possible. The present system — though designed to alleviate the problem of long-term unemployment — serves to prevent people from dropping out of the unemployment benefit system rather than reducing the risk of being trapped in long-term unemployment.

1.2.4. Wage formation and wage flexibility

Wage flexibility is the most important means of adjustment following a shock to the economy. An increase in unemployment normally leads to downward pressure on wages. Therefore, although an accommodating fiscal policy can reduce unemployment in the short term, it may also prevent wage adaptations and thereby aggravate or prolong structural problems as happened in Denmark in the 1970s. However, the wage negotiation process and the social welfare system (including the unemployment benefit system) have also constrained wage flexibility in Denmark.

Wage settlements in Denmark have traditionally stressed solidarity between low- and high-income wage earners. In reality, this has been a 'catching-up' process for low-income wage earners. In Denmark, the unskilled low-income wage earners tend to have most of their salaries determined in the wage settlements, while the higher-paid skilled groups normally only have their base salaries determined in the wage settlements. The higher-paid skilled 'insiders', therefore, have greater scope to negotiate their wages on an individual basis. Bottlenecks in the labour market thus quickly result in high wage increases for key skilled groups of workers; these wage increases ultimately spill over to the whole labour market, as seen in 1986-87 period.

The institutional framework for the wage negotiation process probably plays an important role in wage formation. Wage negotiations in Denmark are centralized to semi-centralized. Normally, a very centralized or a very decentralized system would be considered to be the best to secure a responsible wage development. In a centralized system, it is possible to take unemployment explicitly into consideration from an overall point of view. In a decentralized system, on the other hand, local considerations will dominate. The Danish wage negotiation system has become and will become more decentralized in the future, and this should allow for higher wage flexibility.

The Danish unemployment benefit system and indeed the whole social welfare system has impeded a marked downward wage flexibility for the lower-paid unskilled 'outsider' groups, and thereby also contributed to the relatively high unemployment rate among these groups. The unemployment

benefit system is generous with a very high maximum replacement rate of 90%. There is a maximum ceiling for the benefit payments making it less favourable for high-income groups, but relatively attractive for low-income groups to rely upon unemployment benefits. At the same time, the maximum period in which unemployment benefits are paid is in principle 2,5 years, but is in reality much longer, and as mentioned in Section 2.3 there are few possibilities of forcing people to accept a job offer. Therefore, the system seems to reduce the incentive to work, particularly for the lower-paid wage earners. However, a reform of the benefit system cannot be carried out without including the rest of the social welfare system, since the problem may simply move from one system to the other. This greatly complicates the reform process.

1.2.5. Labour-market reform from May 1993

The government's labour-market reform was a part of the May 1993 fiscal package. Its main element is a reform of the system of passive and active labour-market measures. Concerning the passive labour-market measures, the benefit period will be split in two periods. Period I will have a maximum duration of four years; in this period people will receive an early job offer in order to prevent them from being trapped in long-term unemployment. Period II has a maximum duration of three years, during which the unemployed will have to work, e.g. in social welfare services, in order to receive unemployment benefits.

The active labour-market measures will be restructured and improved in order to accommodate the changes in the passive labour-market measures. The educational efforts for employed and unemployed will thus be strengthened. Furthermore, increased access to leave of absence (up to one year), with the purpose of further education or taking care of one's children, will be provided. People are paid 80% of the normal unemployment benefits during the leave period.

The reform has some advantages in comparison to the current system since it will not be possible to maintain the right to receive unemployment benefits by working in supported jobs or public work-creation programmes. It also aims at providing people with an early job offer, and the unemployed must work, e.g. in social welfare services, in period II in order to receive benefits. The leave of absence possibilities and the strengthening of educational efforts will also improve the qualifications of the labour force and thereby reduce the structural problems on the labour market. Furthermore, as discussed in Section 3.4, a reform of the financing of the unemployment benefit system will be introduced, which it is hoped will contribute to even more responsible wage developments.

The government's proposal has, however, been criticized by professional economists and the employers' federation for not actually including a reform of the benefit system. The unemployment benefit system and indeed the social welfare system as a whole are at the root of many of the structural problems in the Danish labour market.

1.3. Public finances and taxation in Denmark

1.3.1. Taxation and the supply side

The level and structure of taxation affects the supply of production factors. Furthermore, the European internal market makes the harmonization of taxation more important since countries will to a certain extent compete on supply-side conditions for investment. EC harmonization efforts have so far concentrated on indirect taxes.

In Denmark the overall burden of taxation was 48,6% of GDP in 1990 (OECD revenue statistics), which was one of the highest in the OECD area. Rich countries with very high productivity, like Denmark, may be able to sustain higher taxation levels than poorer countries. However, according to an examination of the Danish tax system by a group of independent experts appointed by the government ('the Committee for Personal Taxation'), the present tax system is a major handicap to Danish competitiveness, since the structure of incentives causes a loss of dynamism in the economy. Furthermore, the Danish tax system also differs from that of the other EC countries, particularly with regard to indirect taxes and social security contributions. Thus, adjustments in Danish public finances and taxation seem desirable, if the full benefits from the internal market are to be reaped.

The following sections discuss Danish public finances and the different components of the Danish tax system in view of the challenges stemming from closer European integration. Public finances and the social security system are first analysed, and the tax system is then discussed. An analysis of capital income taxation is not provided. Company earnings are taxed at a rate of 34% in Denmark, but capital income taxation is an extremely complicated matter, and it is outside the scope of this study to provide a full comparison with the rest of the Community.

1.3.2. Public finances and the Danish social security system

Fiscal policy has been relatively tight in recent years with public spending on a declining trend, mainly due to a reduction in the number of central government employees; however, as seen from Table 1, Danish public expenditure is considerably higher than in Germany, and EUR 12.

Danish public expenditure is dominated by transfers to households, which constitute 32% of total public expenditure and almost half of the total central government budget. For example, the State finances two thirds of unemployment benefits while employers and employees finance only one third. The balance of public finances is thus very dependent on the development of transfers. A reduction in cyclical unemployment would cut the public deficit considerably, since the public sector has to cover the entire marginal expense of a rise in unemployment. The budgetary impact of automatic stabilizers is one of the most significant among Community Member States due to the high level of transfers and taxation.

Studies have shown that the Danish social security system is generous by international standards. Low-income earners are compensated relatively well compared to high-income earners, giving transfers a more redistributive function in Denmark than in other countries, but also providing less incentives to job search. Furthermore, access to social transfers like unemployment benefits and pensions is relatively easy.

It appears desirable to increase incentives to work and to start new companies. At the same time, the Danish Welfare State has never been questioned. Thus, the authorities face a dilemma in attempting to lower the tax pressure, since it could imply cuts in the well-developed social security system, in order to ensure a sound development in public finances.

Table 1

Public expenditure, consumption and tax pressure in Denmark and other countries, 1992

			(% of GDP)
	Denmark	Germany[1]	EUR 12
Total expenditure, general government	59,2	48,8	49,8
Public consumption, general government	25,2	18,1	18,4
Tax pressure	49,7	42,8	41,3

[1] West Germany.
Source: Commission services.

1.3.3. The Danish tax system

In Denmark, direct taxes are a relatively more important source of revenue than in the other EC countries. As seen from Table 2, direct taxation as a percentage of Danish GDP is relatively higher, whereas the revenue from social security contributions is at a much lower level than in Germany or EUR 12. The Danish social security system is almost entirely financed by tax revenues.

Table 2

The tax system in Denmark and other countries, 1992

(% of GDP)

	Denmark	Germany	EUR 12
Revenue from:			
Direct taxes	29,8	12,6	12,5
Indirect taxes	17,2	12,9	13,5
Social security contributions	2,7	17,3	15,2
Other current receipts	6,9	3,7	3,6
Total current receipts	56,6	46,5	44,8

Source: Commission services.

The burden of direct taxation is not as high as one would expect, even though the tax rates are higher than in other European countries. For example, there are only small differences in the level of gross and net wages in Denmark compared to Germany, indicating that on average the burden of Danish direct taxation including social security contributions does not deviate substantially from Germany. However, taking indirect taxes into consideration, it is clear that real disposable income is significantly higher in Germany.

The tax rates and particularly the top marginal tax rate is higher in Denmark than in the other EC countries, but the progression of the tax system is not as steep as one might expect (see Table 3). This is *inter alia* due to the possibility of deducting interest expenditure from personal income before tax. However, even though the progression is not as steep as one would expect, high marginal tax rates are a serious problem, since they reduce the incentive to work. These problems are illustrated by the difficulties in attracting foreign experts to work temporarily in Denmark. In recognition of this problem, a law has recently been passed whereby foreign experts working in Denmark for a limited period of time pay only 30% in direct taxes on their gross income.

Social security contributions affect incentives differently than taxes on personal income. Social security contributions paid by the employers would thus increase incentives. However, introduction of social security contributions must also take cost competitiveness into consideration as the financing of social security contributions by employers affects the cost competitiveness of a country in a negative way unless wages decline correspondingly.

The revenue from taxes on goods and services is also relatively higher in Denmark than in Germany and EUR 12 (see Table 2). Taxes on goods and services as a percentage of GDP amount to 17,2% of GDP in Denmark while the similar figures for Germany and EUR 12 are 12,9% and 13,5%.[1] Almost two thirds of the total revenue from taxes on goods and services stem from value-added tax (VAT). Excise duties also generate a substantial revenue but excises have been lowered successively since 1987 as a preparation for the internal market. With respect to European integration, the harmonization of excises is not as crucial as before although excise duties on tobacco and alcohol are substantially higher than in Germany.

Table 3

Effective marginal tax rates, 1991

(%)

	Gross wages (DKR 1 000)					
	100	150	200	250	300	400
Denmark	49,6	51,1	57,1	68,0	68,0	68,0
Sweden	43,0	51,2	51,2	51,2	63,7	63,7
Germany	50,7	53,5	56,2	59,0	53,2	42,6

Source: Skattepolitisk Redegørelse, 1992.

The EC countries have agreed on harmonizing indirect taxes by setting a minimum standard VAT rate of 15% and a reduced minimum rate of 5% for basic necessities. Denmark has only one VAT rate, which applies to virtually all goods and services including basic necessities. In 1992 the Danish VAT rate was increased from 22 to 25% in order to compen-

---

[1] Exports, which are exempted from VAT, have been the main stimulus to Danish economic growth during the last years. A consequence of the export-led growth is decreasing VAT payments and subsequently deteriorating public finances compared to domestic-demand-led growth. Future growth driven by domestic demand could increase the share of indirect taxes.

sate for the abolition of a special social security contribution levelled on the VAT base. The European Court of Justice found that this tax violated an EC VAT directive, and it was thus abolished.

The EC VAT directives do not prevent Denmark from maintaining its present rate of VAT. More compelling could be the market pressure to reduce the rate. From 1 January 1993, the standard German VAT rate has been increased to 15%. The difference of 10 percentage points (18 on basic necessities) leads to substantial savings on some consumer goods when bought in Germany. In the first months of 1993, a flourishing trade with border areas in Germany took place. However, the situation has normalized, and experience since 1 January 1993 suggests that a 10% difference in VAT rates does not give rise to excessive border trade.

A reduction in the VAT rate would have to be accompanied by increases in other taxes or cuts in public expenditure. A simulation on the official Danish econometric model was conducted in the previous Danish country study (April 1991) and a brief review of the major transmission channels and the macroeconomic consequences are described in Box 2. As seen, the short-term implications of a VAT reduction are a substantial increase in economic activity, but the long-term macroeconomic consequences are mainly negative, since the current account and the public-sector balance deteriorate.

Environmental taxes could provide new sources of revenue, which would make a lowering of direct or indirect taxes possible. In Denmark, a CO_2 tax has been introduced, for example. It is at the moment primarily imposed on households while the production sector has obtained widespread exemptions from the tax. This would seem inappropriate as it is equally important that not only the consumption sector is taxed but also the production sector, if positive environmental effects are to be achieved. On the other hand, this kind of tax has to be introduced at EC level in order to avoid distorting the competitive position of the production sector among Member States, and no decision has yet been reached at EC level.

Today, environmental taxes generate a revenue of DKR 1,2 billion but according to an examination carried out by a government-appointed committee of experts (the Committee for Personal Taxation) a reduction in direct taxes in the order of DKR 7 billion financed by environmental taxes is possible. However, the efficient use of environmental taxes could also imply falling tax revenues after a certain period as companies try to find alternative production processes in order to avoid the environmental tax.

1.3.4. The tax reform from May 1993

The Danish Government included an extensive tax reform as part of the May 1993 fiscal package. The reform has the following main elements: a reduction of marginal tax rates, introduction of social security contributions to cover unemployment benefits, active labour-market measures and sick-leave payments. The tax reform will be fully implemented in 1998. The loss of revenue from the reduction of marginal taxes will not be fully compensated by other sources in the initial years, and the tax reform will therefore lead to a reduction in the overall tax burden, and provide a fiscal policy stimulus to the economy in the first years. However, the reform will only amount to a redistribution of taxes when fully implemented in 1998.

Marginal taxes, including the new social security contributions, will range from 43,5% for incomes of less than DKR 130 000 to 62,5% for incomes above DKR 235 000 in 1998 (amounts in 1994 levels). The marginal taxes will therefore be reduced by 7 percentage points for lower incomes and 6,5 percentage points for higher incomes. The labour-market contributions will be levied on gross income and will amount to 8% for the employees and 0,6% for the employers in 1998. However, the labour-market contributions will be adjusted, if for example unemployment increases. Therefore, a link between the payment of labour-market contributions and unemployment is created. This is hoped to contribute to even more responsible wage developments. All in all, Danish marginal taxes should in 1998 be lower than German marginal taxes for the lowest incomes, but about 5 percentage points higher for the highest incomes.

Environmental taxes will gradually be increased in the next five years, particularly on petrol, coal, electricity and water. The new environmental taxes will primarily be levied on households, since the enterprise sector would lose competitiveness if taxes on enterprises were to be increased unilaterally by Denmark. This is, for example, the case for the CO_2 tax, where increases for the enterprise sector will await EC agreement on such taxes.

The tax reform also includes a number of minor measures such as the abolition of a tax on the increase of equity capital in public limited companies and a reduction of the sales tax on shares. Furthermore, fringe benefits will be taxed more heavily, taxation of goodwill will be introduced, and profits on sales of commercial property and shares will be taxed. Particularly, the taxation of profits on shares has been criticized, because it will hit small to medium-sized family-owned enterprises very hard.

1.4. Industrial position and development prospects

1.4.1. Structural changes in the 1980s

The purpose of this section is to analyse the Danish industrial position and the prospects for industrial development from the perspective of industrial structure. The analysis will, therefore, give some indications for employment-creation prospects. The focus is on manufacturing and market services with the exception of financial services, which are treated in Section 5. It is especially a challenge for Denmark as a small, open economy with a particular industrial structure to maximize the benefit from the integrating European economy.

In the following section, the changes in the competitive position in the last years are analysed. Focus is on productivity and relative labour cost developments as well as non-cost factors of particular importance in the internal market, like the size structure of companies, the recent wave of mergers and acquisitions and the degree of internationalization. The second section discusses the industrial development prospects. The analysis is partly based on case-studies of the food products, textile and clothing, pharmaceuticals, sea transport, shipbuilding, and business service industries (see Chapter 3). These are key industries in Denmark.

1.4.2. The competitive position of Danish industrial firms

Due to wage moderation and healthy productivity increases, nominal unit labour costs in Denmark decreased relative to main trading partners after the wage hike in 1987 (see Graph 5). The currency turbulence in the second half of 1992 led to a deterioration in competitiveness, which was particularly pronounced in the big Swedish and British markets; nevertheless, the relative nominal unit labour cost position is still as strong as in 1990 compared to most of the main trading partners, and it is not too unfavourable even in comparison with Sweden and the UK (see Chapter 3 for a further discussion). Denmark has a high cost level, but productivity growth is strong, so that on average Denmark does not seem to have a cost disadvantage.

However, non-cost factors may be a source of competitive weaknesses. In the internal market, scale economies will become more important. This might be a weakness and a barrier to growth, since Danish industry consists mainly of

small to medium-sized companies in international terms. Big companies are often thought to have a key role in the growth process, because they have the potential to act as 'industrial locomotives' gathering a cluster of sub-suppliers around them. It has, for example, been estimated by the Danish Ministry of Finance that one additional job in the biggest Danish manufacturing companies creates 1,9 jobs in other Danish companies. Therefore, the size structure of Danish industry may prove to be a growth barrier in the internal market. There are indications, on the other hand, that a sizable share of all job creation has taken place in small to medium-sized companies.

Changes in company strategy, designed to meet the challenges of the internal market are mergers and acquisitions (M&As) as well as further internationalization. Such strategic moves would lead to larger and more international companies and would be reflected in statistics on M&As as well as foreign direct investment flows.

Foreign direct investment statistics indicate that Danish industry strengthened its international market position at the end of the 1980s and beginning of the 1990s. The process was significant, but not one of revolutionary change. This is probably due to the high degree of internationalization already achieved by the mid-1980s. Many quite small companies have significant and widespread export activities. The extent of the internationalization of Danish industry is evident in the weight of external trade in the economy. Total exports amounted to 37% of GDP in 1990. The biggest markets are the Community and the EFTA countries, which account for about 55% and 20% of exports respectively.

As with other EC countries, Denmark experienced a wave of mergers and acquisitions at the end of the 1980s and beginning of the 1990s. This has led to an important strengthening of key competitive positions, as for example in dairy and meat products, but this development has neither created really big multinational companies (the biggest manufacturing company is Carlsberg with about 14 000 employees) nor changed the overall size structure.

Some Danish companies will probably have to adapt their strategies further in response to the integrating European economy, for example by increasing their specialization. However, it cannot be concluded that the absence of big Danish multinational companies will be a disadvantage in the internal market. Company size is not in itself a competitive advantage. Companies need an optimal size for the strategies they pursue, and the internal market will also facilitate a further internationalization of small to medium-sized firms as is discussed in Section 4.3. Denmark has a

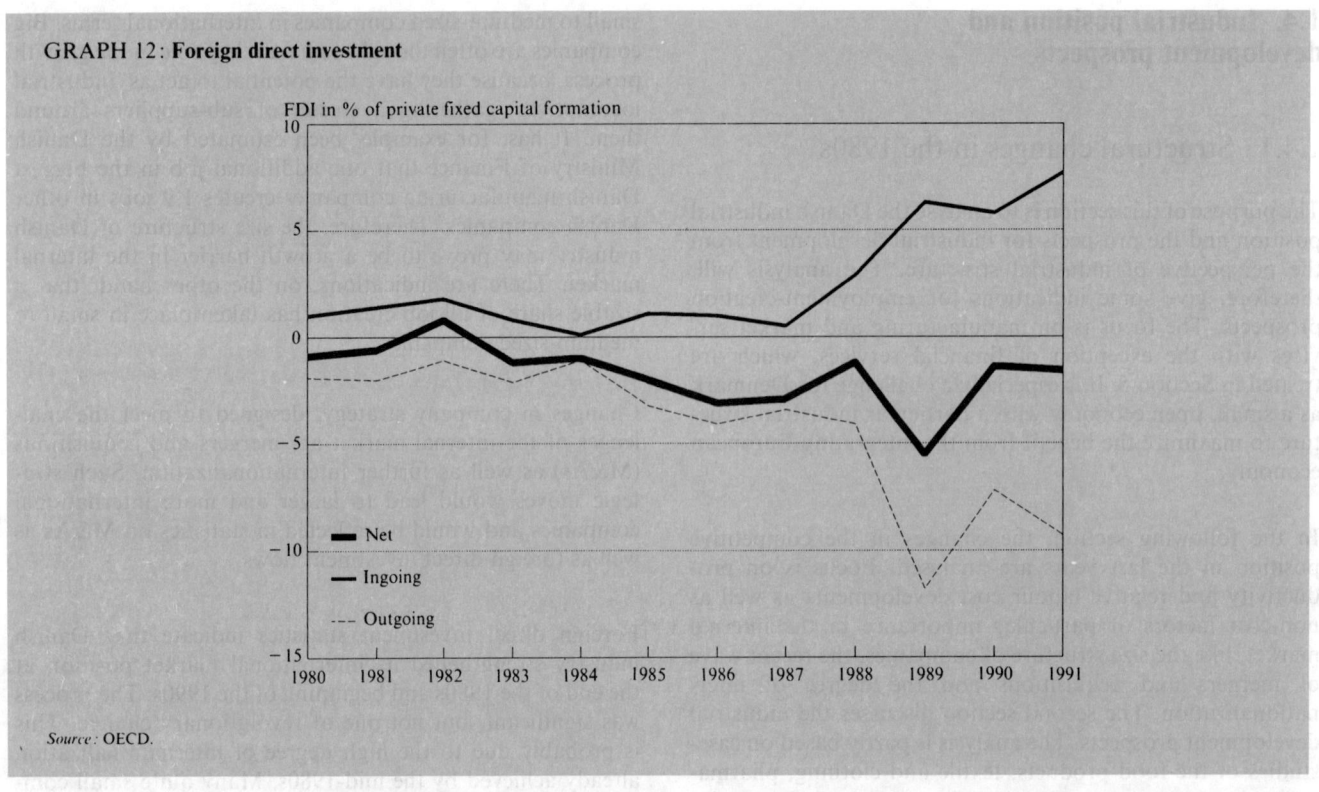

GRAPH 12: Foreign direct investment

FDI in % of private fixed capital formation

- ▬ Net
- — Ingoing
- --- Outgoing

Source: OECD.

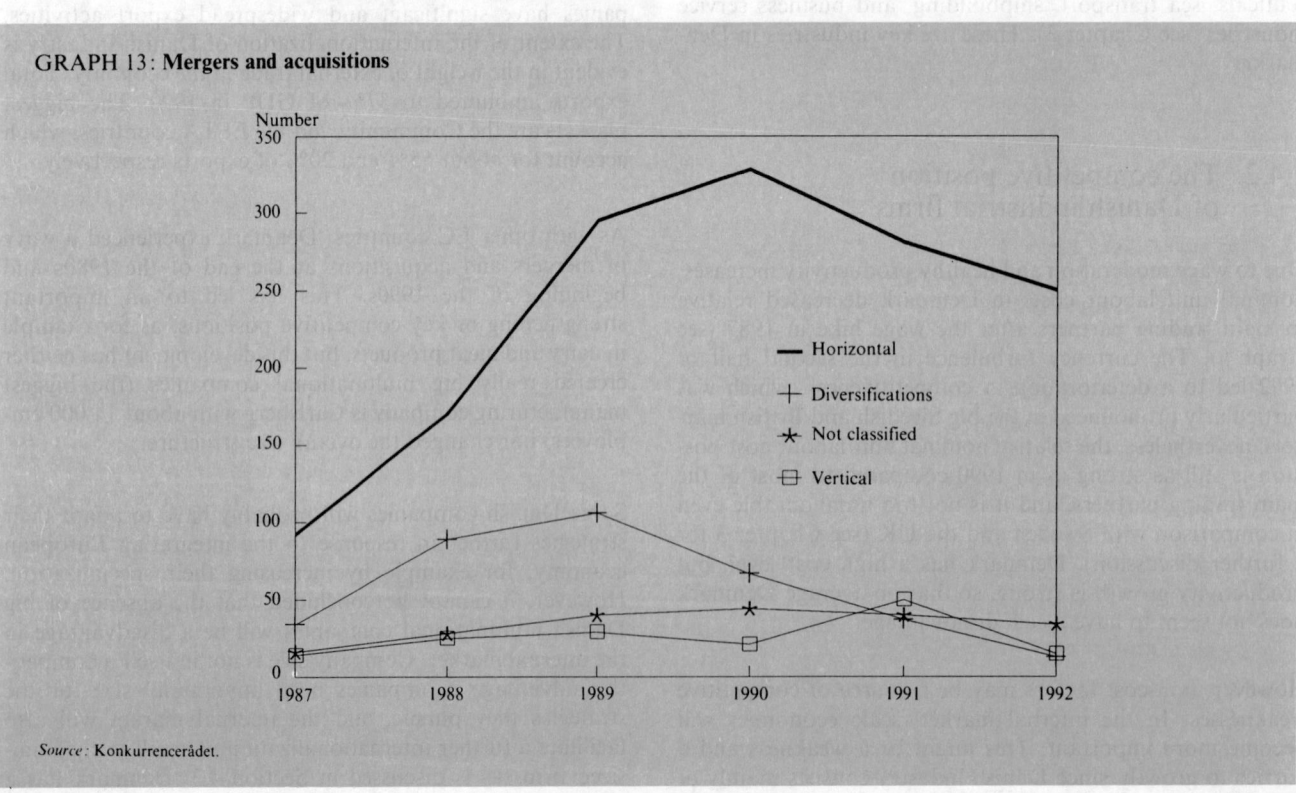

GRAPH 13: Mergers and acquisitions

Number

- ▬ Horizontal
- + Diversifications
- ✳ Not classified
- ⊟ Vertical

Source: Konkurrencerådet.

very efficient industrial sector, and the overall competitive position must be evaluated as quite favourable. The question is rather which opportunities for industrial development and employment creation exist.

1.4.3. Industrial development prospects

The Danish manufacturing sector has its strongest competitive position in relatively mature industries like food production, shipbuilding and furniture. Denmark also has a strong position in pharmaceuticals, which is a high-growth industry, but the presence of so-called 'high-tech — high-growth' industries is generally modest. Therefore, the industry structure would in itself seem to imply modest economic growth prospects. However, Danish growth prospects in mature industries may be quite different from the European or global average. Danish food products, shipbuilding, shipping, and textile industries are examples of industries which have been able to prosper through innovation and entrepreneurship.

Denmark spends considerably less on research and development (R&D) measured in terms of GDP than many other OECD countries. The relatively low level of R&D could potentially lead to a weakening of the Danish economy, since innovation is a more important factor than cost in trade between industrialized countries. However, R&D is not only a question of the available amount of money, but also how R&D funds are spent. It would not be a solution simply to boost R&D and try to develop strong positions in some high-tech areas with strong growth potential. It is difficult for a small country to commit the resources necessary to participate in mainstream high-tech industries. A company like IBM spends more on R&D than countries like Denmark, Belgium and Australia. Research and development of course plays a key role in industrial development, but rather than focus on 'high-tech — high-growth' industries it would seem advisable for Denmark to strengthen its research in areas where strong positions have already been achieved. An example of such an effort is a recent research programme in food technology. The programme involves cooperation between different research institutions and companies from the food sector, and is the first research programme to be administered by several ministries. In addition to a strengthening of existing mature industries, it may, of course, also be possible to develop some high-tech niche industries.

From an overall point of view, Danish manufacturing industry seems to have good prospects. However, the long-term employment-creation prospects are uncertain. From the point of view of industrial structure, it is unlikely that

employment will increase in the largest companies. Many of the largest companies have achieved dominant positions on the home market. Further rationalization seems likely, and this would create a tendency towards a decline in employment, at least in the domestic economy. The trend towards higher specialization could mean that exports from the large companies will increase. However, these companies are already highly specialized and have high exports.

The somewhat negative employment-creation prospects in the larger companies may be counterbalanced by the small to medium-sized business sector. The internal market should open many opportunities for small to medium-sized companies to specialize further and, for example, become sub-suppliers to larger foreign companies. In this way, the internal market can help Denmark to overcome a structural deficiency. It is, therefore, important to further reduce barriers to new company formation and to growth of small to medium-sized firms. The Danish Government has, for example, established a 'network' programme to promote cooperation between smaller companies, but it is still too early to judge the results of the programme.

The service industries probably have a greater potential than manufacturing industries to become major providers of new jobs. This is, to a large extent, simply a continuation of existing trends, where increasing real incomes and leisure time will increase the demand for cultural activities, travel, sports activities, etc. Furthermore, the ageing of the population will increase the demand for health services, and there may also be particular service areas which are underdeveloped due to tax or labour-market structures. Studies by the Danish Ministry of Finance have, for example, shown that there is a potential for job creation in household services through a reduction of 'do-it-yourself labour' and the black economy. The reason is that the high marginal tax rate of 68% and high minimum wages make it very expensive for householders to buy household services since the high wages have to be paid from income, which has been taxed at 68%. Furthermore, the potential for a black economy is quite high under these circumstances. However, it is difficult to estimate the potential number of new jobs which could be created.

In discussing services and employment generation, particularly in connection with the creation of high-productivity jobs, the interrelationship between services and manufacturing also has to be considered. The Danish sea transport, shipping and shipbuilding industries are, for example, dependent on each other for their competitive advantage and represent the two main 'pillars' in the Danish maritime industrial complex. A similar relationship exists in health care and pharmaceuticals. There is a potential for creation of high-productivity jobs by strengthening such interrelationships.

All in all, it can be concluded that, from the point of view of industrial structure, Denmark is in quite a good position to profit from the integrating European economy. To achieve beneficial effects, greater specialization will be necessary, and it will become more important to attract investment, which aims at using Denmark as an export base. At the moment, there are indications that a large part of foreign direct investment in Denmark has been made in order to serve the Danish home market (*Industri og Handelsstyrelsen*, February 1993).

The location at the periphery of the internal market could, to some extent, be a disadvantage since the core of the Community (often said to be South-East England, the Benelux, southern and western Germany, northern France, northern Italy, as well as the Madrid and Barcelona regions) will become a more attractive location. The problem is that the internal market will lead to a cut in trading costs, and this may favour utilizing scale economies, achievable in the core regions. Lower wage costs could counteract this effect, but Denmark is a high wage cost country.

There is, however, no reason to be too pessimistic in this respect. True, Denmark is at the moment at the periphery of the Community, but on the other hand it has close links to the rest of Scandinavia, and is relatively closely located to industrial centres in Germany and Sweden. Denmark should also benefit from the re-establishment of its historic links to the Baltic and Eastern European countries. In this sense, Denmark does not really belong to the periphery.

Furthermore, the investment decisions of companies are based not only on cost considerations, but also on the existence of a favourable industrial environment, for example in terms of the availability of sub-suppliers, well-qualified labour and a good infrastructure. In this respect, it is important to strengthen existing industrial complexes, since this will create stronger and more attractive industrial environments, which can facilitate the energizing of growth clusters in the Danish economy. However, such an approach should not imply subsidies or interventionist industrial policies, but simply the creation of a more favourable environment for companies. The opportunities from a regional point of view may therefore be quite good, if the implementation of supply-side policies oriented towards exploiting the integrating European market are continued.

1.4.4. The measures for furthering industrial development from May 1993

Industrial development is influenced by a wide range of general conditions. The changes in the tax system and the

labour-market reform mentioned in Sections 2.5 and 3.4 are in themselves very important for industrial development prospects.

However, as part of the May 1993 fiscal package the Danish Government also included various other measures to strengthen industrial development. It is thus proposed to increase efforts to educate and provide guidance to entrepreneurs as well as to increase the subsidies for developing the product ideas of entrepreneurs. Furthermore, the R&D efforts in food technology will be strengthened.

The most significant new measure, in terms of budgetary outlays, is a new proposal through which it is planned to boost the purchase of household services. In a trial period of three years, services provided by private companies to private households can be supported through wage subsidies. This is expected to create a significant number of new jobs, primarily for unskilled labour.

Furthermore, a number of planned infrastructure investments have been brought forward. Significant new investments are thus planned for the railways, and a number of other investments, for example roads, have also been accelerated over the last year. A few high-profile projects are also under way: Denmark is currently building a bridge/tunnel across the Great Belt, and a bridge/tunnel across Øresund between Denmark and Sweden is under preparation as a Danish/Swedish joint venture.

1.5. The financial sector

1.5.1. Institutional changes and recent difficulties

Over the past several years, the Danish financial system has evolved rapidly to face the challenges posed by financial integration in Europe and the substantial alterations in the domestic legislative framework. Traditional demarcation lines between individual categories of financial institutions have increasingly become blurred and collaboration across the spectrum of financial service providers is becoming the norm.

Perhaps the most significant changes have come about in the banking sector. The distinction between savings and commercial banks disappeared in 1989, with savings banks being permitted to become limited liability companies, thus removing the last remaining difference between the two types of operations which had been allowed to conduct the same kinds of business since 1975. In addition, major mergers took place at the end of the 1980s to form two large domestic banking groups, accounting for over half the assets of all banks, but only ranking 40th and 50th in overall European terms. The mergers have brought about quite significant rationalization in terms of the numbers of bank branches in the country and employment in the industry, as has the progressive decline in the number of smaller banks. However the visions of large Danish or Scandinavian financial conglomerates appear to have receded as the sector has been buffeted by increases in bad-debt provisions and declines in asset quality. As has been the case internationally, Danish institutions have progressively begun to concentrate more on their core business, pulling out, sometimes at substantial cost, from ancillary activities and scaling back their expansion into foreign markets where share has often been built up by taking on business rejected by already established institutions.

The more specialized mortgage credit institutions, which help to make the Danish bond market the world's ninth largest, have also been hit by difficult economic conditions, in particular in the property market.

Insurance companies are also feeling the effects of deterioration in asset quality, in particular at holding-company level due to the ill-fated merger and diversification attempts of the early 1990s. The interests of policy-holders have not, however, been endangered as the insurance subsidiaries have — with minor exceptions — remained healthy, with premium income remaining buoyant and investment risk being circumscribed by the relevant prudential regulation.

However, in terms of the difficulties being experienced in other Scandinavian markets, Danish financial institutions are in far better shape. This is generally because of better capitalization, closer supervision and earlier liberalization in the cycle. Since own capital requirements for Danish banks were already significantly tighter than recently established international standards, Danish banks are not faced, as certain institutions are elsewhere, with the difficulty of strengthening capital ratios in a period of economic sluggishness. Margins have, however, become tighter and the banking system is faced with the necessity of cutting back operating expenditure. This has been a slow process despite the rationalization possibilities opened up by the mergers. To some extent it also leaves the way open for greater incursions by foreign financial institutions, whose presence in Denmark is at the moment very minor (two foreign subsidiaries and six foreign branches in 1992), in niche markets. For instance, as the traditional banks cut back on services and become less omnipresent at local level, customers may move towards other banks with even more

restricted services but offering tighter interest-rate spreads. Although this development is already under way domestically in Denmark, it should be noted that it has been the model for foreign banks breaking into markets in a number of European countries. Such a development would undoubtedly slow down the return to profitability of the main banking groups.

In addition, the active encouragement of firms raising money abroad since the early 1980s, witnessed by a sharp increase in business loans booked abroad in the first half of the 1980s may have narrowed the lending possibilities of the domestic banking system and fostered a reliance on external financing by large Danish corporations, although often taking place through Danish banks operating abroad. To a certain extent this may have led to some contraction in the captive market of the Danish financial system.

1.5.2. Employment-creation prospects

The capacity of the financial sector to create the increased employment opportunities necessary for the Danish economy seems to be extremely limited in the next few years. The adjustments to meet changed conditions have resulted in very considerable staff reductions in the past few years and it is likely that labour shedding will continue to be a major factor in the sector over the next two or three years. All categories of the financial sector seem to be equally affected by this consolidation effort with particular emphasis on the necessity of cut-backs being felt in insurance, banking and mortgage credit institutions. Some compensatory employment opportunities could emerge, however, in the area of investment services as the expansion of the activities of the Danish stock exchange, presaged by the increasing attractiveness of the exchange, modernization and the introduction of derivatives, place Copenhagen at the forefront of developments at a regional level and in a position to draw business from other Scandinavian exchanges. However, it is considered unlikely that this will prevent an overall decline in the employment in the financial sector.

1.6. Conclusions

As a small, open economy, Denmark is facing several macro- and microeconomic challenges in the process of European integration. Not only does Denmark face strong limitations in the conduct of its macroeconomic policies, but particular emphasis must also be put on the implications of some special features of the Danish economy such as its highly developed social benefit system and the structure of its enterprise sector. The present country study tries to throw some light on these economic challenges in order to assess Danish economic prospects in the process of economic and monetary integration.

On the macroeconomic level, Denmark has successfully implemented a policy devoted to nominal stability. The inflation rate is persistently low, public finances have been under control, and the current-account balance exhibits a solid surplus after a long period of deficits and accumulating external debt. However, the overall picture is considerably darkened by a period of slow growth since 1987 and continuously rising unemployment up to a level of 12,4% (August 1993).

Economic policies were geared to achieving and safeguarding a large degree of nominal stability. While monetary policy was credibly devoted to maintaining the strong currency policy in the ERM, fiscal policy successfully prevented any significant slippage in terms of a higher deficit and some progress was made towards harmonization of indirect taxes within the Community, a crucial issue in Danish economic policy. The primary aim of economic policies was to improve medium-term growth conditions by gradual but continuous supply-side reform and to regain external competitiveness, which was lost after the 1987 wage slippage, by moderate increases in unit labour costs.

Wage developments have been consistent with the stability-oriented strategy of improving growth conditions by gradually increasing profit margins and external competitiveness. Not only has nominal wage growth declined with declining inflation, but real unit labour costs steadily declined, a sound profit situation was established and external competitiveness was improving from the late 1980s until the second half of 1992. Wage settlements have increasingly taken into account the serious consequences of excessive wage increases in a regime of quasi-fixed nominal exchange rates.

Reducing unemployment is the biggest challenge in the Danish economy. A significant part of Danish unemployment is due to weak demand. A revival of both domestic and external demand is crucial in reducing unemployment. However, structural problems persist in the labour-market, preventing unemployment from falling to a low level. Any strategy to reduce unemployment will therefore have to address both the short-term cyclical problems as well as the medium- to long-term problems related to labour-market structures and industrial development.

In the short run, revitalizing domestic demand could be a major factor in boosting growth and reducing unemployment. Exports have been the principal impetus to growth in recent years, while domestic demand has been weak. The large surplus on the current account seems to provide room for some expansion of domestic demand. High real interest rates have been a major factor in constraining private sector demand, and the current situation calls for an easing of domestic monetary policy. The Danish Government introduced a fiscal stimulus in May 1993. The package includes measures reforming the tax system and the labour market as well as some new industrial development measures. The aim is to achieve both growth and structural reforms. The Danish Government expects the package to cause only a minor deterioration of the budget deficit.

A durable solution to labour-market imbalances will only be possible if structural unemployment can be reduced, which implies making labour-market structures, including wage formation, less rigid. Structural impediments in the Danish labour market exist in the wage formation process, the wage structure, the unemployment benefit system, and the social welfare system. Easy access to fairly generous unemployment benefits, for example, has reduced the incentive for labour search, in particular among less-qualified workers. In the case of Denmark, there is little doubt that the very high activity rate is also a consequence of the social security system.

The structural problems in the labour market threaten to introduce a structural component to the budget deficit which has so far been the result of conjunctural factors. Structural problems have also been causing a misallocation of resources. The relatively generous unemployment benefit system in combination with liberal firing rules have sometimes been exploited by enterprises in low-production periods. Furthermore, a relatively compressed wage structure and a high minimum wage have reduced the demand for unskilled labour. The reform of the unemployment benefit system included in the government's fiscal package from May 1993 aims at reducing structural impediments.

A substantial reduction in unemployment will require not only that structural problems on the labour market are reduced, but also that additional jobs are created. An improvement of both cost and non-cost competitiveness is necessary in order to achieve a rate of growth that can, in the medium term, reduce unemployment. It is in this respect important that the Danish enterprise sector is in a good position to profit from the integrating European economy. The recent government measures will be supportive in this respect since R&D are strengthened and marginal taxes reduced. However, the overall tax pressure is only temporarily reduced, since additional environmental taxes will be introduced in 1996 to compensate for the loss of tax revenue.

There is no reason to be too pessimistic about long-term employment-creation prospects in manufacturing. The experience of the 1983-86 boom showed that jobs were created in a wide number of industries during an economic up-turn, but, from a structural point of view, job-creation prospects are limited in manufacturing, where mature industries are dominant. Furthermore, prospects for additional job creation in the largest Danish companies are bleak, since many of these companies have dominant positions on the home market, and are strong in mature industries. The potential for new job creation is higher among small to medium-sized companies and through new company formation. Particularly, the internal market should open possibilities for further internationalization and specialization of small to medium-sized companies. However, from a structural point of view, employment-creation prospects are better in the services sector. It is difficult to predict exactly which sectors will grow, but the Danish consumption of household services is, in an international comparison, at a rather low level, and there seems to be a potential for job creation through an increased consumption of household services as well as a reduction of the black economy — if the cost of such services could be reduced. A new government initiative included in the recent fiscal package aims at increasing employment in this sector through wage subsidies.

An increased effort to attract foreign direct investment will be important in the integrating European economy. In general, the degree of specialization of companies is expected to increase, and it would therefore be desirable to attract companies which would use Denmark as an export base. The openings in Eastern Europe as well as the prospects of the other Nordic countries entering the Community should help in making Denmark a more attractive place in which to invest, but in order to capitalize on these opportunities it is necessary to continue to invest in education, R&D, and infrastructure.

Overall, Denmark is in a good position to profit from the integrating European economy and to reduce unemployment in the medium term, if structural improvements are achieved, but it will probably be necessary to live with high unemployment in the short term. An export-led recovery was anticipated in the early 1990s and first signals of the success of the medium-term oriented strategy were emerging. However, the weak international conjuncture and exchange-rate movements have hampered this economic policy strategy. Although a weak labour-market performance was helpful in fostering wage adjustments, unemployment has now increased to a record high level.

Box 1: Monetary developments

Monetary policy instruments, interest rate

Monetary and liquidity policy instruments are geared towards influencing the central Danish money-market rates and, thus, the interest-rate differential *vis-à-vis* corresponding rates abroad. During the course of 1991, interest-rate differentials between the krone and other narrow-band currencies in the ERM were significantly reduced. Against this background, the Nationalbank considered it necessary to be able to manage the interest-rate differential in a more accurate way. In April 1992, the Nationalbank introduced a new set of monetary and liquidity policy instruments in order to influence the central Danish money-market rates in a more gradual and flexible manner. The main liquidity policy instruments are now sales and purchases of certificates of deposit (CDs) issued by the central bank and treasury-bill/government-bond repurchase agreements.

The interest rates set by the Nationalbank on CDs and repurchase agreements are the most important rates for steering the Danish money-market rates. Since April 1992, these rates have been changed quite often in response to developments in the foreign-exchange market. The discount rate remains the overall indicative rate of interest for changes in monetary policy. This was increased by 150 basis points to 11% on 4 February 1993, in response to heavy speculative attacks against the krone in the foreign-exchange markets. After continuous foreign-currency inflows, the discount rate was gradually brought down to 9,25% by the end of April, and was further reduced after the 'yes' to the Maastricht Treaty in the referendum on 18 May 1993 to a level of 7,25% at the beginning of July. When ERM tensions re-emerged, the discount rate was again increased, but has subsequently been reduced gradually to a level of 7,75% by mid-October, following the stabilization of the exchange rate.

The ERM turmoil

The consistent hard currency policy followed by Denmark since 1982 paid off in terms of lower inflation and lower interest-rate differentials *vis-à-vis* the German mark. By the second half of 1991 the three-month interest-rate differential between the Danish krone and the German mark had been virtually eliminated. From late 1991 onwards, however, this favourable trend was broken. Widening of differentials emerged: first, as a result of tensions in the ERM in November and December 1991, which also put the Danish krone under pressure in the foreign-exchange market; later, in the aftermath of the 'no' to the Maastricht Treaty in the referendum in June 1992; finally, as a result of repeated speculative attacks against the Danish krone during the recurrent ERM turmoil in the final months of 1992 and in 1993. The Danish krone has, therefore, been strongly affected by the ERM turmoil despite Denmark's sound economic fundamentals.

The hard currency policy enjoys a high degree of political consensus, and the Danish authorities have demonstrated great willingness to use interest rates to defend the exchange-rate parity. Furthermore, nominal fundamentals have remained strong. All these factors should strongly underpin the credibility of Denmark's exchange-rate commitment. Nevertheless, the persistent high interest-rate differential *vis-à-vis* the German mark in late 1992 and several periods of 1993 compared to pre-September 1992 levels, suggests that the markets have seriously questioned Denmark's exchange-rate commitment.

Several factors may explain the apparent inconsistency between the underlying economic fundamentals and the fortunes of the krone during the ERM turmoil:

(i) The impact of the Danish referendum raised doubts whether Denmark would continue to participate fully in the Community. The Edinburgh Summit in December 1992 should have erased such doubts, even though these may have still played a role until the second referendum on 18 May 1993.

(ii) The dented credibility of the ERM in the financial markets affected the credibility of all currencies not clearly seen as belonging to the very 'hard core' of the ERM. Denmark's preference not to participate in Stage III of the EMU possibly also affected the markets' view of the Danish krone in this respect. The show of firm support for the krone from other ERM central banks coupled with the Bundesbank's cut in interest rates during the ERM turmoil in early February 1993 may, however, have changed this perception; the stability of the krone during the realignments of the peseta and the escudo within the ERM in May 1993 also indicate such a change in perception.

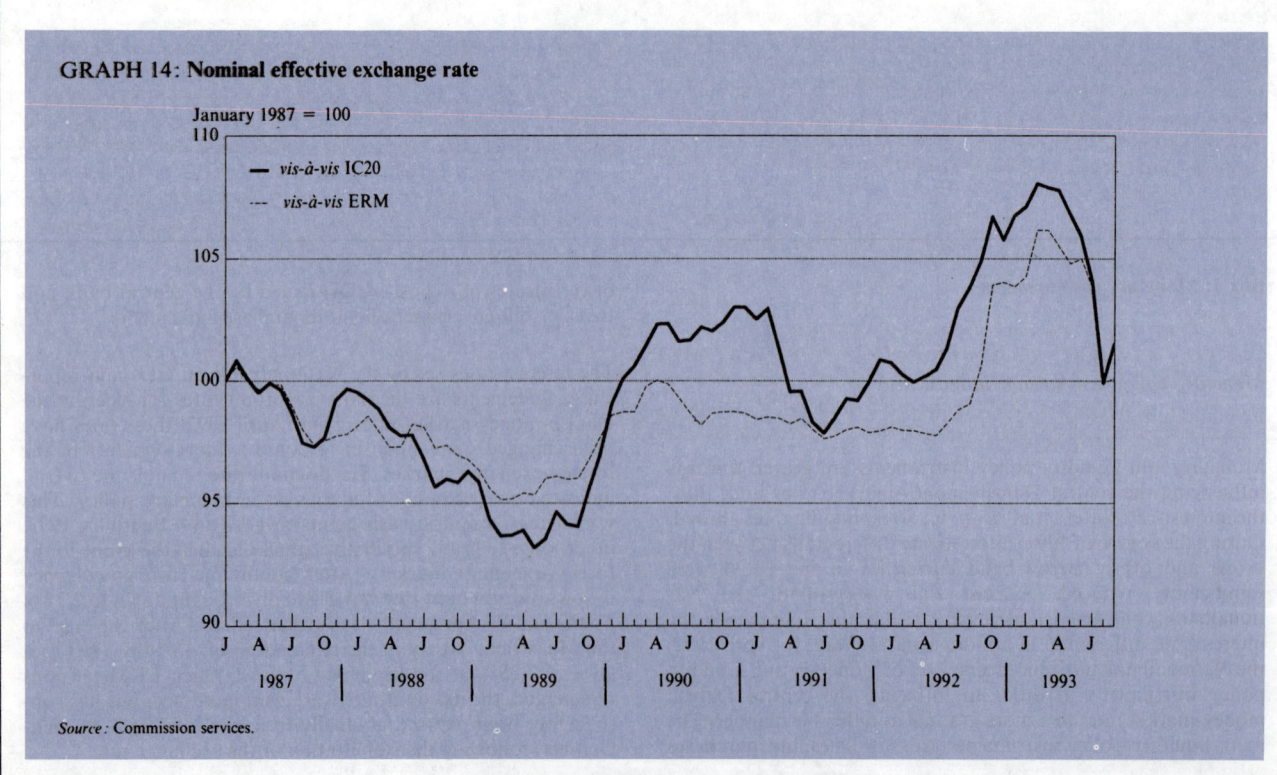

GRAPH 14: **Nominal effective exchange rate**

January 1987 = 100

— *vis-à-vis* IC20

--- *vis-à-vis* ERM

Source: Commission services.

(iii) After having gained competitiveness in real terms in the period 1987-92, Denmark was hard hit by the ERM turmoil in terms of loss of competitiveness. In the period September to December 1992, currencies having a combined weight of more than a third of Denmark's effective exchange-rate index had either to devalue or to float. As measured by the nominal effective exchange rate *vis-à-vis* IC20 (20 industrialized countries), the krone appreciated by more than 7,2% from the first half of 1992 to March 1993. Denmark's short-term loss of competitiveness, including the impact of the depreciation of the formerly ecu-linked Nordic currencies (the depreciation of the Swedish krone was the single most important factor behind the nominal appreciation of the Danish krone in 1992), did perhaps focus the markets' attention on the persistently high unemployment rate. Indeed, with recession deepening in a number of ERM countries, the markets assessed the monetary policy stance and high real interest rates implied by the ERM commitment as untenable. As a result, tensions in the ERM re-emerged in July 1993 and by the end of the month the krone, the French and Belgian francs as well as the Iberian currencies came under pressure. Following this, it was decided to widen the bilateral fluctuation margins within the ERM to approximately 15%.

Box 2: Effects on the Danish economy of reducing indirect taxes

A simulation of the effects on the Danish economy of reducing indirect taxes was conducted in the April 1991 country study. In the simulation, the VAT rate on basic necessities such as food products, non-alcoholic beverages, etc. was reduced from 22 to 9%. The reduction in the VAT rate was estimated to lead to an immediate budgetary loss of about − 1,2% of GDP. Including harmonization of excise duties, where Denmark today is in much better compliance with EC directives as a consequence of the easing of excise duties on a wide range of products, the harmonization of indirect taxes would have a budgetary impact of − 2,2% of GDP. A simulation was then conducted analysing the impact on the main economic variables by cutting indirect taxes by 2,2% of GDP.

A cut in indirect taxes causes downward pressure on wages in the short term via lower consumer prices. The ensuing reduction in unit labour costs leads to a further reduction in consumer prices. The drop in consumer prices causes a rise in real disposable income and a substantial increase in private consumption. As a consequence, the trade balance and the current account deteriorates due to higher growth in imports than exports. The public sector balance is in deficit the first two years but becomes positive in the third year as economic activity and private consumption gain momentum. This improvement is mainly due to a reduction in the rate of unemployment and transfer payments. After the first two years, the increase in the level of production and employment leads to higher wage claims which reduces demand by lowering exports. Unemployment then rises and domestic demand decreases. This development has serious long-term implications for the public sector balance, which deteriorates due to falling receipts and increased expenditure, in turn, leading to lower public sector net saving and increasing current-account deficits.

A reduction in the VAT rate thus leads to substantial increases in economic activity in the short term, but the long-term implications are mainly negative. Therefore, the long-term implications necessitate either an increase in other taxes or cuts in government spending.

Chapter 2

Unemployment and the Danish labour market

2.0. Introduction

In comparison with the rest of the Community the Danish unemployment rate was relatively low in the 1980s, since it was on average only 7,6% compared to 9,6% for the whole Community area measured on standardized rates. However, Danish unemployment was in absolute terms very high and has risen to record levels in recent years. In August 1993 unemployment reached 352 000, and the unemployment rate 12,4% (national definition[1]). The cost of passive and active labour-market measures amounted to close to 8% of GDP in 1992 and unemployment benefits alone almost to 4% of GDP.[2] High unemployment is associated with large social cost, heavy tax pressure, and implies that a large share of available resources is not being properly utilized.

A large part of Danish unemployment is structural. The experience from the 1986-87 boom suggests that the NAIRU is about 8% (see Chapter 1, Section 1.1). Specific labour-market groups may play a key role in determining the level of the NAIRU. In 1986-87, bottlenecks developed in construction, and this had spillover effects on the whole economy. Thus, a reduction in unemployment through faster growth in the future could readily trigger inflationary tensions. It is important to combine any growth-stimulating strategy with labour-market reforms in order to reduce the NAIRU, and it would seem advisable to undertake the labour-market reforms before growth resumes. A labour-market reform was passed by the Danish Parliament in June 1993, as will be discussed in Section 4.

The present chapter discusses the nature of Danish unemployment and the structural problems in the labour market. In Section 1, developments in the 1980s in the labour force, employment and unemployment are analysed. In Section 2,

the nature of unemployment, and in Section 3 structural problems on the labour market are analysed. Finally, in Section 4, the implications of the recent labour-market reform are considered in some detail.

2.1. The development in the labour force, employment, and unemployment in the 1980s

Employment increased from 2,4 million to 2,6 million between 1980 and 1990. It peaked in 1987 and has since declined gradually to its current level. At the same time, the labour force increased by 5,9% (from 1980 to 1990) and unemployment from 7% in 1980 to 11,1% in 1992 (see Graph 15). Statistically seen, demographics were the major factor behind the rise in unemployment. In the total population, the number of persons in the group 15 to 66 years of age increased by 4% in the 1980s. There was a relatively large number of youngsters entering the labour force in the 1980s, and migration made a positive contribution to the increase in the labour force. Of the overall 5,9% increase in the labour force in the 1980s, 4,1 percentage points can thus be ascribed to demographics. The activity rate also increased slightly over the decade contributing 1,8 percentage points of the increase in the labour force. The activity rate increased mainly due to a higher activity rate amongst females (see Graph 16). A trend towards more part-time employment would tend to offset the rise in the labour force, but as seen in Graph 16 part-time employment has decreased slightly over the decade.

The developments in employment, labour force and unemployment indicate that a main problem in the 1980s was to create jobs for new entrants to the labour market. In the 1990s the nature of the unemployment problem will change to some extent. The number of people entering the labour market will decrease over the next decade, and the labour force is expected to start declining by the mid-1990s. Furthermore, as seen from Table 4 there will be a shift towards a higher average age of the population between 15 and 64 years, and this will lead to an ageing of the labour force. As discussed below, these developments do not imply that the unemployment problem will somehow be solved automatically, but they will have implications for labour-market policy.

2.2. The nature of unemployment

The official unemployment rate does not provide a complete picture of the extent of the unemployment problem. A number of people participate in active labour-market measures

---

[1]   The numerical difference between the national Danish definition and the Eurostat definition of unemployment is around 1,5 percentage points. The main reason for the difference is the treatment of unemployment spells of short duration. As will be discussed later in this annex, Denmark has many short unemployment spells, which are included in the national, but not the international definition of unemployment.

[2]   It should, though, be noted that Danish unemployment benefits are taxable income, which is not the case in most other countries.

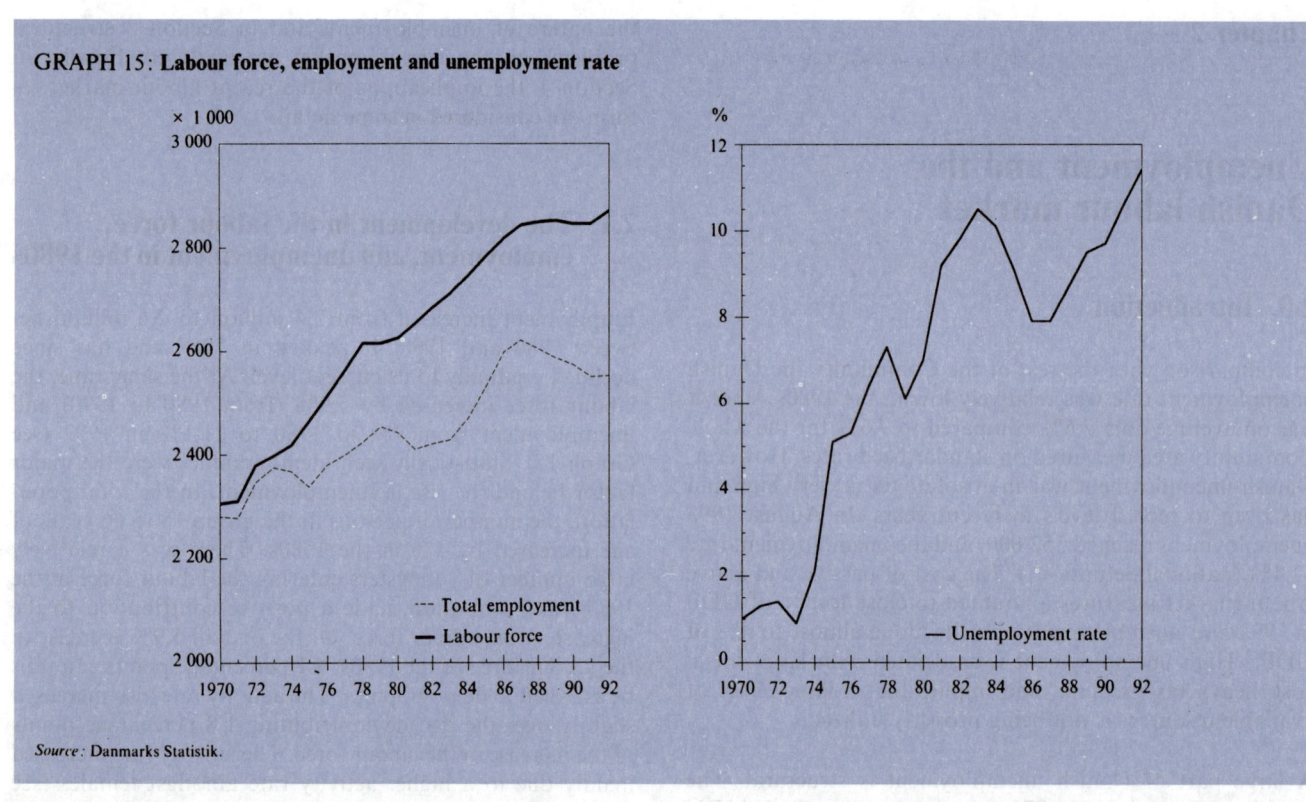

GRAPH 15: **Labour force, employment and unemployment rate**

× 1 000

---- Total employment
— Labour force

— Unemployment rate

Source: Danmarks Statistik.

Table 4

Forecast of population of working age in Denmark, 1992-2002

	1992		1997		2002	
	number	%	number	%	number	%
0-14	875,0	17,0	921,8	17,7	986,5	18,8
15-24	738,3	14,3	666,1	12,8	582,4	11,1
24-49	1 949,6	37,8	1 921,3	36,8	1 895,3	36,1
50-64	795,3	15,4	914,8	17,5	1 011,1	19,2
>64	803,9	15,6	793,7	15,2	781,5	14,9
Total	5 162,1	100,0	5 216,7	100,0	5 257,2	100,0

Source: Danmarks Statistik, Befolkningsprognose, Alternativ 1, Nyt Fra Danmark Statistik,1992.

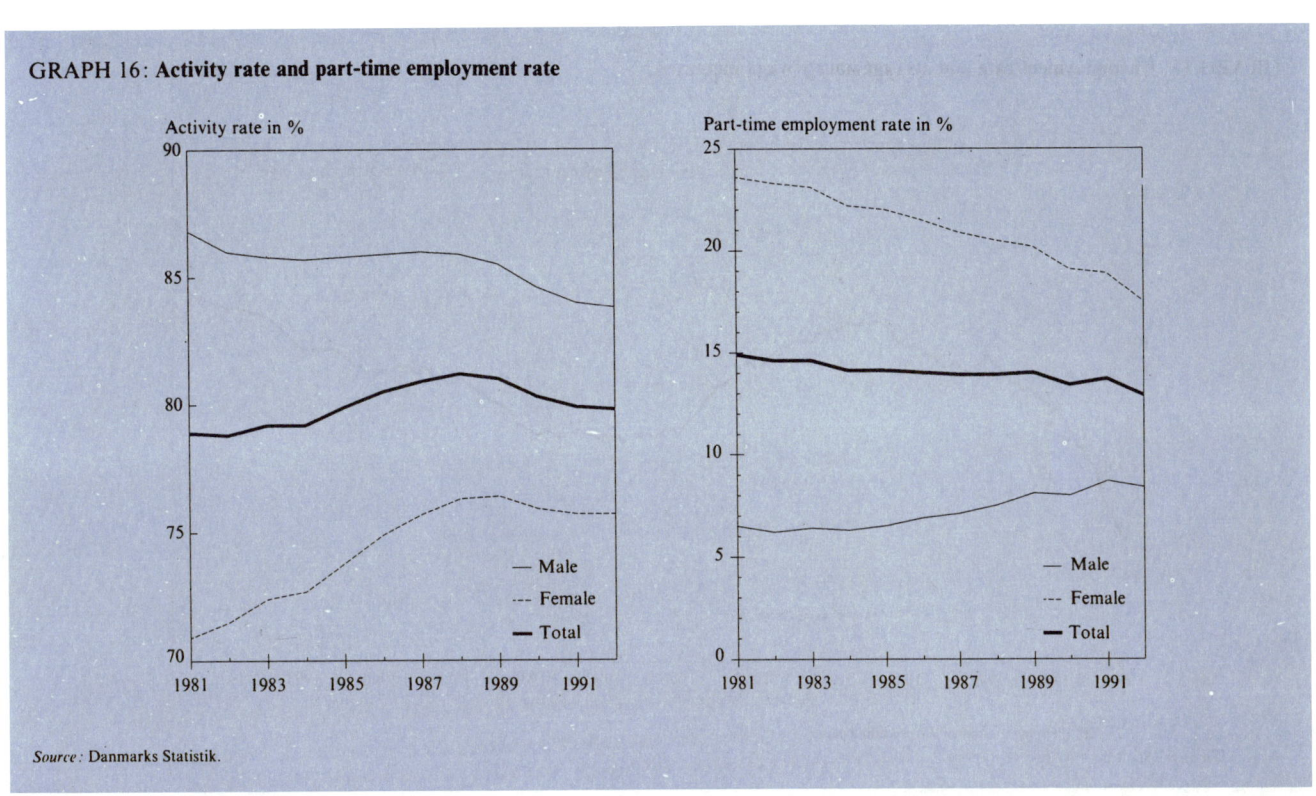

GRAPH 16: **Activity rate and part-time employment rate**

Activity rate in %

Part-time employment rate in %

— Male
--- Female
— Total

Source: Danmarks Statistik.

or are in early retirement. Active labour-market measures encompass offers of jobs particularly created for people out of work for more than a year, unemployment benefits for people taking further education, and unemployment benefit payments for people starting their own business. In total, about 4% of the labour force (including the early retirement scheme) do not have a regular job, but are not officially registered as unemployed.

The major part of official Danish unemployment is structural, but it is difficult to estimate exactly how large a part of unemployment can be ascribed to structural problems and how much is simply due to cyclical factors. As mentioned, in the Danish case the experience from 1986-87, where unemployment decreased due to an increase in domestic demand, provides some guidance and indicates a NAIRU of around 8% (see Graph 17). There are no indications that structural unemployment since has fallen. Calculations in the Danish Ministry of Finance thus indicate a current level for the UCRU (unchanged competitiveness rate of unemployment) of around 8 to 9%. At the most 4 percentage points, or one third of official unemployment, seem to be due to the effects of the business cycle.

The large structural component in Danish unemployment is supported by the shape of the Beveridge curve, which shows the relationship between the number of vacancies and the number of unemployed (see Graph 18). A negative relationship between the number of vacancies and the number of unemployed is a sign that the labour market is functioning normally. Rightwards shifts in the Beveridge curve, for example following a shock to the economy, indicate an increased persistence in unemployment (hysteresis).

The Danish Beveridge curve must be interpreted with some caution since Danish employers do not have to report job vacancies. This figure therefore does not include all vacant jobs, and can only be taken as an indicator of the total number of vacant jobs in the economy. In any case, it is seen that the low-unemployment period at the beginning of the 1970s shows a normal relationship without a shift in the curve. However, since the mid-1970s the curve has shifted rightwards, and most recently it has even shifted upwards to the right. There are therefore signs of an increased mismatch on the labour market or that the unemployed are not as efficient in searching for new jobs as in the early 1970s.

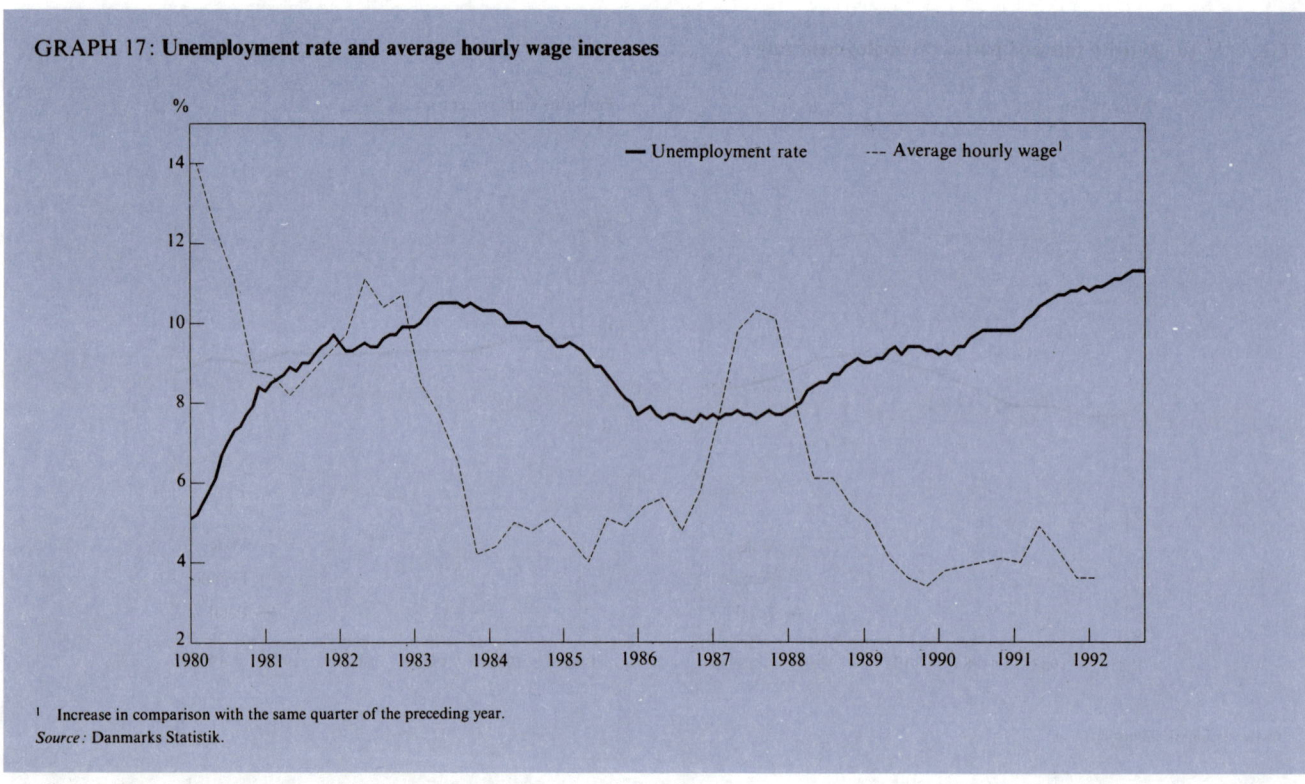

GRAPH 17: **Unemployment rate and average hourly wage increases**

%

— Unemployment rate   --- Average hourly wage[1]

[1] Increase in comparison with the same quarter of the preceding year.
Source: Danmarks Statistik.

The persistence of structural problems on the labour market is also confirmed by the unevenly distributed incidence of unemployment among labour-market groups. As seen from Graph 19 the unemployment rates for youngsters and females are thus higher than for males, even though Denmark has performed better than most other Community countries in terms of youth unemployment. The relatively higher unemployment for youngsters is to some extent a consequence of the relatively large number of young people entering the labour market in the 1980s. The figures in Graph 19 probably underestimate this problem, because of various job-creation programmes targeting youngsters. Furthermore, unskilled workers have a very high rate of unemployment. The two largest trade unions for unskilled workers both have unemployment rates of more than 20% for their members.

The unevenly distributed incidence of unemployment also indicates an insider-outsider problem on the Danish labour market, where the unemployment burden is carried largely by a specific group of people. A core of about one third of the unemployed consists of people who have been out of work for a longer period of time, whereas for some groups

the probability of becoming unemployed is virtually non-existent.

A certain level of unemployment is unavoidable. Frictional unemployment in connection with job changes, for example, causes a natural minimum level of unemployment. As a rule of thumb, it is normally believed that frictions account for about 1 to 2 percentage points of this unemployment rate. This is significant, and it is important to reduce frictional unemployment. However, other factors which are not necessarily unavoidable are important sources of the current high level of structural unemployment.

2.3. Structural labour-market issues

2.3.1. Geographical mobility

Low geographical mobility may lead to a situation with high unemployment in some regions and shortage of labour in other regions. Studies have shown that in Denmark only a

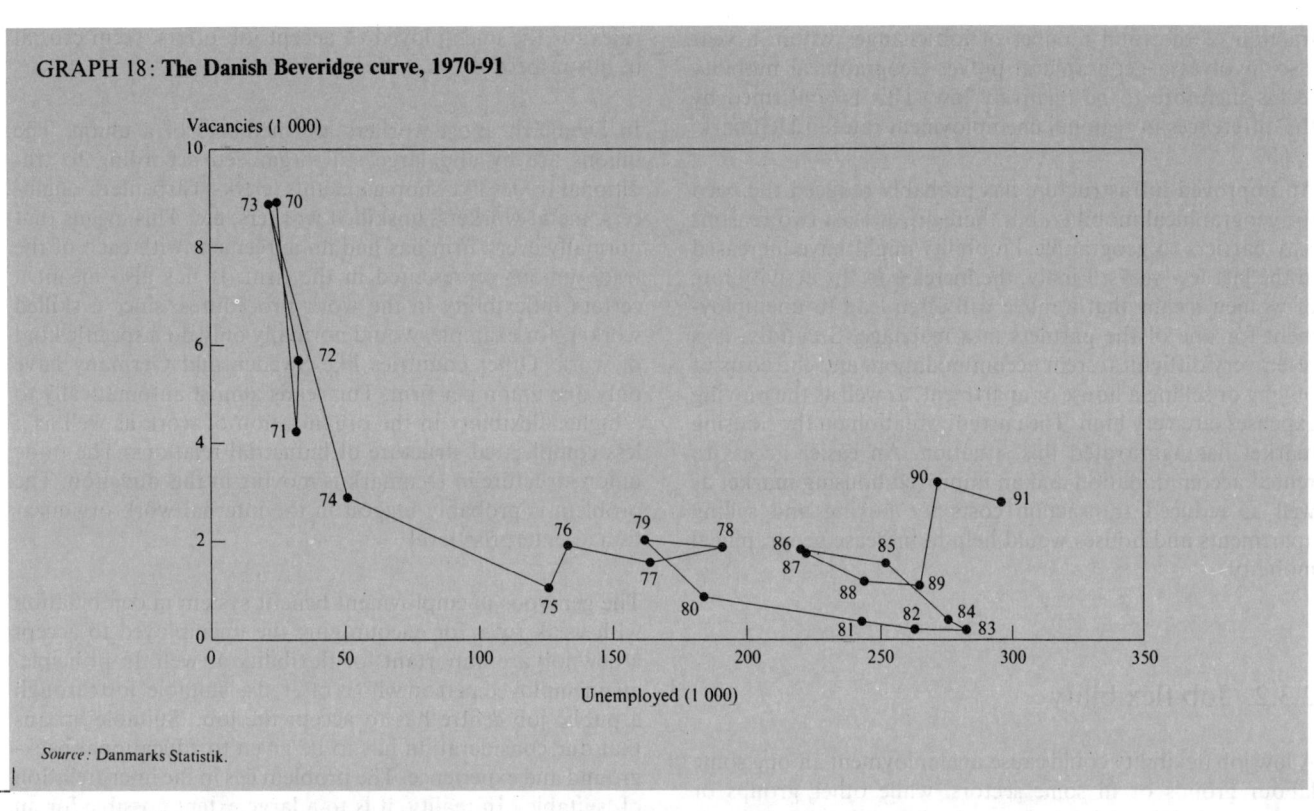

GRAPH 18: **The Danish Beveridge curve, 1970-91**

Source: Danmarks Statistik.

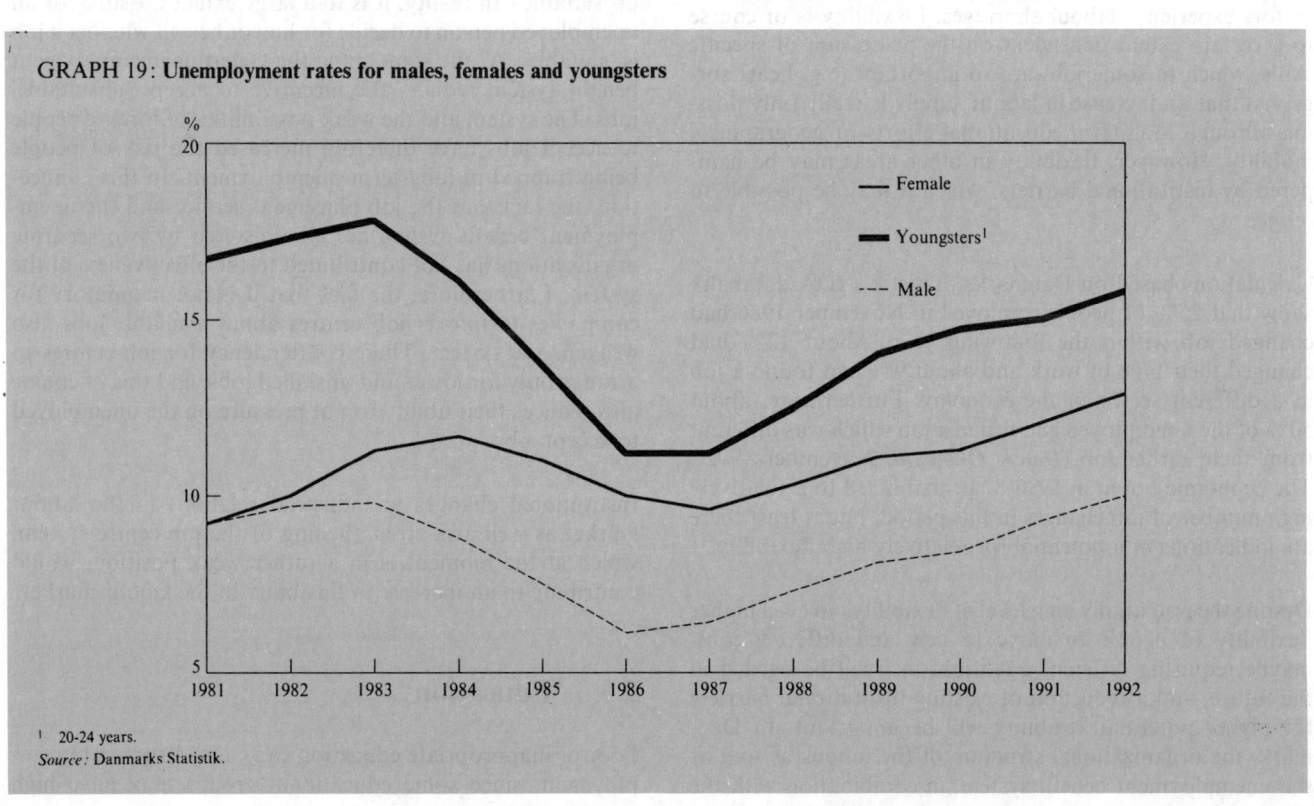

GRAPH 19: **Unemployment rates for males, females and youngsters**

[1] 20-24 years.
Source: Danmarks Statistik.

fraction of the total number of job changes within a year also involves a geographical move. Geographical mobility seems therefore to be relatively low. This is confirmed by the differences in regional unemployment rates in Denmark.

An improved infrastructure has probably reduced the need for geographical mobility, but there are at least two reasons why barriers to geographical mobility might have increased in the last few years. Firstly, the increase in the activity rate of women means that a move will often lead to unemployment for one of the partners in a marriage. Secondly, it is often very difficult to rent accommodation, and the costs of buying or selling a house or apartment, as well as the moving expenses, are very high. The current situation on the housing market has aggravated this situation. An easier access to rented accommodation and an improved housing market as well as reduced transaction costs for buying and selling apartments and houses would help to increase geographical mobility.

2.3.2. Job flexibility

A low job flexibility could cause unemployment among some labour groups or in some sectors, while other groups or sectors experience labour shortages. Flexibility is of course to a certain extent dependent on the possession of specific skills, which in some jobs are so important (e.g. heart surgeons) that an increase in labour supply is really only possible through long-term educational efforts or geographical mobility. However, flexibility in other areas may be hampered by institutional barriers, which it may be possible to reduce.

Calculations based on Danmarks Statistik's IDA databank show that 25% of people employed in November 1986 had changed job within the following year. About 12% had changed their type of work and about 9% had found a job in a different sector of the economy. Furthermore, about 50% of the unemployed had found a job which was different from their earlier job (*Dansk Økonomi*, November 1992). The economic boom in 1986-87 probably led to a relatively high number of job changes in this period, but at least there are indications of a potential for relatively high flexibility.

Despite the potentially high level of flexibility, an even higher flexibility of people to move to new and different jobs, maybe requiring different qualifications, will be needed in the future, and a reduction of existing institutional barriers for higher potential flexibility will be important. In Denmark, the organizational structure of the unions as well as the unemployment benefit system, in combination with the

rules for the unemployed to accept job offers, seem crucial in this respect.

In Denmark, most workers are members of a union. The unions are by and large still organized according to traditional trades like shop assistants, clerks, carpenters, engineers, metal-workers, unskilled workers, etc. This means that normally every firm has had an agreement with each of the trade unions represented in the firm. It has also meant a certain inflexibility in the work procedures, since a skilled worker, for example, would normally only do a specific kind of work. Other countries like Sweden and Germany have only one union per firm. This leads almost automatically to a higher flexibility in the organization of work as well as a less complicated structure of industrial relations. The trade union structure in Denmark is moving in this direction. The problem is probably biggest in the internal work organization at enterprise level.

The generous unemployment benefit system in combination with weak rules for encouraging the unemployed to accept a new job are important for flexibility as well. In principle, an unemployed person who is offered a 'suitable' job through a public job centre has to accept the job. 'Suitable' means that due consideration has to be given to educational background and experience. The problem lies in the interpretation of 'suitable'. In reality, it is to a large extent possible for an unemployed person to decide for him or herself whether a job is 'suitable'. At the same, time the generous unemployment benefit system reduces the incentive to accept 'unsuitable' jobs. The system and the weak possibilities of forcing people to accept jobs have therefore increased the risk of people being trapped in long-term unemployment. In this connection, the fact that the job placement service and the unemployment benefit system are administered by two separate organizations has not contributed to the effectiveness of the system. Furthermore, the fact that it is not mandatory for companies to inform job centres about available jobs also weakens the system. There is a tendency for job centres to arrange only for lower and unskilled jobs, and this of course also reduces their ability to put pressure on the unemployed to accept jobs.

Institutional changes in industrial relations in the labour market as well as a strengthening of the job centre system, which at the moment is in a rather weak position, would contribute to an increase in flexibility in the labour market.

2.3.3. Education

Poor or inappropriate education can cause structural unemployment, since some educational groups may have high rates of unemployment, while a shortage of labour exists for other educational groups. Such mismatch problems can be reduced through education. In addition, education tends to increase a person's mobility and flexibility.

In general, the educational level of the Danish labour force is very high. About 16% (1990) of the population has undergone higher education, while only about 28% (1990) has had no further education after primary school. There has been an upgrading of the educational level of the population over the last decades. More people are receiving an education and particularly more people are receiving a higher education. Therefore, the younger part of the population tends to have a higher level of education than the elderly.

Overall, the Danish educational system is probably one of the best in the world. It has seen several improvements in the 1980s, including an expansion of the school system for education of skilled labour, and an expansion of formalized Ph.D. programmes. Another important policy change has been the greater emphasis on technical, economics, management, languages and business education. Improvements have been introduced, but a continued upgrading of the educational system is essential in order to stay competitive in the internal market.

At the moment there are no bottlenecks in the labour market, but a NAIRU around 8% prompts the question of which requirements in terms of education, training and retraining programmes are needed. The upgrading of the educational level of the population will in itself tend to reduce the risk of bottlenecks occurring in the labour market since education increases the potential for flexibility and mobility. However, in order to reduce the risk of a mismatch on the labour market it would of course be preferable if the resources were channelled to those skills most needed in the future. On the other hand, this is dependent on sectoral developments, and the future demand for labour is therefore not easy to estimate. The private service and manufacturing industries do not, for example, demand exactly the same type of education, and the future relative size of these two sectors is therefore in principle important for educational policy.

Furthermore, greater emphasis on continued education for people already in the work-force will be necessary in the 1990s. First of all, the ageing of the work-force and the decline in the number of new entrants to the labour market will make it necessary to channel more resources to continued education of people already in work. Secondly, technological development and higher internationalization will also increase the need for continued education. It will be increasingly necessary to view a career as an educational process. The recent labour-market reform points to some extent in this direction (see Section 4).

Further education for people in the work-force will be relevant for all groups on the labour market. However, since unskilled workers are particularly exposed to unemployment, special measures for them would seem warranted. A reform of the existing educational system for unskilled workers is currently being considered.

2.3.4. Active labour-market measures

Long unemployment spells tend to reduce the productivity of labour and therefore increase the risk of people being trapped in unemployment. Active labour-market measures encompass financial incentives for unemployed persons to become entrepreneurs or to undertake education, as well as specific offers of jobs or education. Denmark spent about 1,1% of GDP on active labour-market measures in 1992. This percentage is one of the highest in the OECD.

Job-creation measures, for example supported labour, constitute most of the active labour-market measures. Denmark thus spent around 0,5% of GDP on job-creation measures in 1992. Despite the substantial active labour-market efforts a NAIRU of 8% indicates that the resources are not utilized as effectively as could be wished.

A big problem is that the current system is primarily designed to prevent people from dropping out of the unemployment benefit system. The rules for offering people a job mean that the unemployed often first receive a job offer shortly before they would lose their unemployment benefits. After having been in a supported job for nine months (the required minimum to be able to continue to draw unemployment benefits), many people return to the unemployment benefit system. There have also been examples of the system being used by firms to hire cheap labour. A firm would simply hire an unemployed person for nine months and receive a wage subsidy. At the end of the nine months' period the person is then fired and a new unemployed person is hired.

Clearly a reform of the system would seem desirable. A system which has its main emphasis on securing peoples' right to draw unemployment benefits instead of reducing the risk of being stuck in long-term unemployment does not seem to be the best way to utilize the available resources nor to reduce structural unemployment. Rather, a system designed to meet the individual needs of the unemployed at an early point in the unemployment period would seem inappropriate. This point is clearly recognized in Denmark, and experiments with new and more decentralized active labour-market measures have begun in 1993, and it is a part of the recent labour-market reform (see also Section 4).

2.3.5. Temporary layoffs and the unemployment benefit system

In Denmark unemployment caused by temporary layoffs is a particularly important problem. A committee of experts appointed by the Danish Government estimated temporary layoffs to account for about 0,5 of a percentage point of total unemployment, but this is probably a low estimate.

The reason for the high number of short-term unemployment spells is in particular the relatively easy firing of people combined with a generous unemployment benefit system. Several sectors, like the fishing industry and the harbours, have been able to use the unemployment benefit system to a certain extent as a buffer by temporarily laying people off in periods with low demand. This has enabled some companies to achieve a relaxed production planning. There have even been examples of companies (for example, producers of agricultural machines) locating their cyclically sensitive production in Denmark, because of the possibility of using the benefit system as a buffer.

The additional expenses to unemployment benefit payments are significant, but the costs of misusing the system in this way are not simply higher expenditure for unemployment benefits, but also a less rational utilization of the work-force, since companies tend to tie up a larger labour force than necessary. Furthermore, it will also make the economy more sensitive to cyclical developments, if cyclically sensitive production is favoured.

Some measures have been introduced in order to counter the problem: the unemployment benefit system was modified to give temporarily laid-off workers lower benefit payments with the employers having to pay the unemployment benefits of the first two days of unemployment. These measures have tended to reduce the abuse of the system.

A further tightening of the system, for example by making the employers' contributions to the unemployment benefit system dependent on the number of people they have fired over a number of years, as known from the United States, could be considered. However, in this connection it should also be noted that liberal firing regulations are of particular importance in Denmark due to the predominance of small to medium-sized firms in the Danish industrial sector.

2.3.6. The wage formation process

A high rate of unemployment is normally assumed to lead to wage moderation. General economic policies can therefore have an important impact on the wage formation process. Thus, in the 1960s and 1970s Denmark had an accommodating fiscal policy, i.e. fiscal policy was used actively to reduce unemployment following an external shock to the economy. An accommodating fiscal policy leads to a short-term decrease in unemployment, but does not accommodate a longer-term adaptation of wages. Private sector employment was therefore crowded out. From this perspective it would seem essential to have tight fiscal policies in order to maintain the current macroeconomic regime and to prevent private sector employment from being crowded out.

In wage negotiations, the Danish trade unions have traditionally stressed the importance of wage solidarity between the various labour-market groups. This has lead to a relatively high minimum wage as well as an attempt to let the wages of the lower-paid, often unskilled, labour groups follow the wages of the higher-paid and often skilled labour groups. However, in reality the solidarity of the stronger insider groups on the labour market with the weaker lower-paid outsider groups may not be that high. The skilled labour groups on the Danish labour market have a large element of decentrally negotiated pay in their wages. Therefore, wage increases for the lower-paid groups have often served to catch up with the higher-paid groups.

The policy has been somewhat successful in reducing the spread of wage differences, leading to a relatively compressed wage structure, but as a consequence of the wage increases unemployment has risen for the relatively less productive, unskilled labour groups. The social welfare and unemployment benefit systems have also been important factors in this respect, preventing downward wage flexibility (see Section 3.7 below).

The Danish wage formation process is set to become more flexible, since wage negotiations are expected to become more decentralized in the future. For the time being, the Danish wage negotiation process is semi-decentralized. This may also to a certain extent explain the lack of solidarity between the higher-paid insiders and the lower-paid outsiders on the labour market, as witnessed in the excessively high salary increases experienced in 1987, at a time when unemployment was still very high. The structure of the wage formation process contributed to very high general salary increases even though these were not warranted by the high level of unemployment.

A semi-decentralized system such as the current Danish system does not seem to be the best way to secure 'responsible' wage developments. A highly centralized as well as a highly decentralized wage negotiation process are both believed to lead to the rate of unemployment having a strong influence on wage increases. In a highly centralized system the trade unions will have a big incentive to take the state of the economy and the public finances into account. In a highly decentralized system on the other hand, it would be expected that local considerations would play an important role. However, in a semi-decentralized system, the consequences of damaging wage increases are not as transparent, and unemployment will therefore not have as big an influence on the wage formation process. The crucial question is of course whether the 1987 experience would have been less pronounced if the wage formation process had been more decentralized.

2.3.7. Wage flexibility, the social welfare system and the unemployment benefit system

The structure of the Danish social welfare and unemployment benefit systems is a crucial factor behind low wage flexibility. Firstly, the unemployment benefit system has a maximum replacement ratio of 90% and a ceiling on benefit payments thus making it less attractive for high-income groups, but very attractive for the lower-paid groups to draw benefits. This is even more the case if the effect of the distribution of other transfer income, like support for child care and housing aid, is included. The incentive for lower-paid groups, for example, to accept a job with lower wages than a former job is reduced through these arrangements. Furthermore, the unemployment benefit system allows people to draw unemployment benefits for up to two and a half years, but effectively the period can be much longer.

Secondly, the financing structure of the unemployment benefit system implies that the marginal risk of an increase in unemployment is carried solely by the government, and not by the employees or the employers. In addition, research has shown that wages are by and large determined by the groups with the lowest risk of unemployment, i.e. the insiders. Therefore, the cost of an increase in unemployment is not directly affecting wage negotiations. The link between the financing of unemployment benefits and wages seems to be weak.

Thirdly, the Danish social welfare and unemployment benefit systems have a direct and major impact on wage structure and thereby structural unemployment. The generosity of

the systems has contributed to a rather compressed wage structure with a high minimum wage. Therefore, the differences in wages are smaller than the differences in productivity for the various educational groups on the labour market, and, as a consequence, it is the low-skilled labour groups who have the highest rates of unemployment. Many lower-grade jobs in for example the service industries have undoubtedly disappeared due to a compressed wage structure with a relatively high minimum wage. Overall, a reform allowing for greater downward wage flexibility, particularly for youngsters and others with a relatively low productivity, seems appropriate.

The wage structure in turn also creates problems for the entry of young people into the labour force. In some cases, it is more attractive for young people to be unemployed or to work as unskilled labour than to enter education. In other cases, the relatively high minimum wage has also discouraged employers from hiring inexperienced young people rather than more experienced people. A special entry salary for young people will be introduced in 1993, and this should reduce the problem.

Overall, it must therefore be concluded that the structure of the Danish social welfare and unemployment benefit systems is a main factor behind the lack of wage flexibility on the Danish labour market. However, changing the system will be a very complex task, since simply making the unemployment benefit system less generous might lead to a shifting of problems to other parts of the social system.

2.4. The recent labour-market reform

In June 1993 the Danish Parliament passed a labour-market reform in order to deal with some of the problems mentioned in Section 3. The reform contains three main initiatives.

Firstly, it includes a reform of the whole system of passive and active labour-market measures. The unemployment benefit period is split into period I with a maximum duration of four years, and period II with a maximum duration of three years. In period I, a personal action programme for the unemployed is made after three months of unemployment. The intention is then to give the unemployed an early job offer in order to prevent long-term unemployment. The unemployed person has to accept all activating measures included in his or her action programme. In period II, it is intended to offer activating measures throughout the whole period — on average 20 hours per week. The idea is to let the unemployed work for the unemployment benefits they receive. Secondly, educational efforts are strengthened. Thirdly, it introduces a flexible access to leave of absence for up to one year while maintaining the right to draw 80% of the normal unemployment benefits. The leave of absence can be used for further education or child care.

The reform aims at reducing structural unemployment and has a number of improvements compared to the current system:

(i) educational efforts are strengthened, improving skills and flexibility;

(ii) the strengthening of educational efforts and the leave-of-absence reform create better room for activating measures;

(iii) it will not be possible to earn a right to stay in the unemployment benefit system by working in various employment generation programmes, e.g. supported jobs;

(iv) it will provide people with an early job offer in period I and thereby reduce the risk of being stuck in long-term unemployment;

(v) the unemployed have to work throughout period II.

Furthermore, as mentioned in Section 3.4 of Chapter 1, the reform of the financing structure of the unemployment benefit system will create a link between unemployment and contributions to the unemployment benefit system. However, the government's proposal has been strongly criticized by professional economists and the employers' federation, particularly because it does not actually include a reform of the unemployment benefit system.

2.5. Conclusions

As a rough estimate, structural unemployment accounts for about two thirds or 8% of the Danish labour force and Danish expenditure on labour-market measures amounts to almost 8% of GDP. However, the existing labour-market measures do not seem to have worked well in the sense that they have not been able to reduce structural unemployment.

Room for structural improvements exists in several areas. It will be crucial to increase flexibility and mobility. Investment in education will be important in this respect, and particularly continued education for people in the work-force will become more important due to the ageing of the labour force, more rapid technological changes and increasing internationalization. Furthermore, a reform of active labour-market measures, more flexible industrial relations, and a strengthening of the job-placement system would also increase flexibility.

However, it would also seem decisive to reduce the problems associated with temporary layoffs and to increase wage flexibility. Equally crucial in this respect would seem to be a reform of the unemployment benefit system, which as discussed above, is to a certain extent misused and inhibits flexibility.

The current structural labour-market problems will make it difficult to achieve high sustainable economic growth and thereby reduce unemployment without endangering the current macroeconomic regime. At the moment there is some room for recovery in the Danish economy, but sustainable high growth is only feasible if structural labour-market problems are confronted. The recent labour-market reform deals to a certain extent with these problems.

References

Bjørn, N. H., Pedersen T. M., 'Insiders and outsiders in the Danish labour market', working paper from the Secretariat of the Danish Economic Council, 1992.

Dansk Økonomi, The Danish Economic Council, Copenhagen, June 1988, June 1990, May 1992, November 1992.

Finansredegørelse 92, The Danish Ministry of Finance, April 1992.

Finansredegørelse 92, Bilag, The Danish Ministry of Finance, April 1992.

Gelting, Thomas, 'Geografisk mobilitet i arbejdsstyrken', *Arbejdsnotat* No 4, Danmarks Statistik.

Hvidbog om arbejdsmarkedets strukturproblemer, May 1989, The Danish Ministries of Labour, Finance, Taxation, Social Relations, Education, and Economic Affairs.

Viby-Mogensen, Gunnar (ed.), *Kampen mod Ledigheden,* Rockwool Fondens Froskningsprojekt, Spektrum, 1992.

Pedersen, Peder J., 'Omfanget af arbejdsmarkedspolitiske Foranstaltninger, 1971-89', working paper, Centre for Labour Economics, University of Aarhus and Aarhus School of Business, 1991.

Rapport fra Udredningsudvalget om arbejdsmarkedets strukturproblemer, Udredningsudvalget, June 1992.

Sørensen, Troels, 'Arbejdsløshed − 90'ernes udfordring', *Arbejdsnotat* No 5, Danmarks Statistik.

Uddannelsesbetingede tilpasningsbehov på arbejdsmarkedet, The Danish Ministry of Education, May 1990.

Udspil til reformer på arbejdsmarkedet, the Danish Government, April 1993.

Chapter 3

Industrial position and development prospects

3.0. Introduction

The objective of this chapter is to make a qualitative analysis of the medium- to long-term growth prospects of the Danish industrial sector from the point of view of industry structure. This is particularly relevant in view of the establishment of the internal market. The industrial sector is here defined as manufacturing and market services, excluding financial services, which are treated in Chapter 4.

The medium- to long-term growth prospects will depend on competitiveness. In macroeconomics, competitiveness is normally discussed in terms of relative labour cost. However, non-cost factors are important as well. A better way to examine the problem of competitiveness and industrial development, rather than simply looking at relative labour cost, is to focus in a more global way on the development in the competitive positions of a country's industries.[1] The question is especially whether existing competitive industry positions have been strengthened in preparation for the internal market, and what the possibilities are for expanding existing as well as creating new market positions.

In the first section the overall structure of the Danish economy and structural developments in the 1980s are discussed. In the second section the competitive position of Danish industry is analysed. Particularly, the relative cost position, the size structure, the recent wave of mergers and acquisitions and the degree of internationalization of Danish industry are discussed in order to make an overall assessment of the changes in international market positions. In the third section the prospects for industrial development are analysed, partly by drawing on a number of industry cases. The cases are described in the appendix to this chapter.

---

[1]   Non-cost factors of particular relevance for competitiveness in the internal market are the size structure and the degree of internationalization of companies. The problem of developing new competitive industry positions is, however, a question of entrepreneurship. Industrial policy has a key role in creating a well-functioning framework for entrepreneurial activities.

3.1. Structural developments in the 1980s

Before the Danish industrial revolution in the second half of the 19th century, the main industries were sea transport and particularly farming. The industrial revolution in the second half of the 19th century led to the development of a large manufacturing sector, and the relative importance of farming declined. In the 1970s the relative importance of manufacturing also began to decline, and the service industries became more important. It has been argued that manufacturing will experience the same development as agriculture, thus leading to a movement towards a post-industrialized service society. This is probably true, but manufacturing will continue to be a key sector in the Danish economy for many years.

The development in industry structure in the 1980s in many ways simply represents a continuation of the trends of past decades. As seen from Table 5, the relative share of agriculture as a percentage of GDP continued to decline from 5,6 to 4,5%. The share of manufacturing fell from 20,4 to 18,5%, whereas market services increased from 44,2 to 48,8%. Public services remained largely constant, but the number of public employees has increased. An important but seemingly small change in industry structure is the growth in mining. This reflects the increase in the production of North Sea oil and gas, which for the first time made Denmark a net exporter of oil and gas in 1991.

Overall, Denmark has experienced a development similar to other advanced industrialized economies, where service industries make up an increasing weight in the economy. However, Denmark deviates in two important respects from other industrialized countries. Firstly, the manufacturing

---

Table 5

Sectoral distribution of GDP at factor cost (current prices)

		(%)
	1980	1990
Agriculture, forestry, fishing	5,6	4,5
Mining	0,1	1,1
Manufacturing	20,4	18,5
Power, gas and heating	1,4	1,9
Construction	7,7	6,4
Market services	44,2	48,8
Non-profit-making organizations	0,7	0,7
Public services	22,9	22,0
Imputed financial services	−3,1	−3,9
Total	100,0	100,0

Source: Danmarks Statistik, national accounts.

sector has never accounted for as big a share of GDP as in many other industrialized countries, and, secondly, the creation of a modern Welfare State led to a relatively larger public sector than in most other Western countries. Those were important factors behind the chronic current account deficits from 1963 until 1990 (see country study, April 1991).

3.2. The competitive position of Danish industrial firms

3.2.1. The development of cost competitiveness in the 1980s

As discussed in Chapter 1 (see Graph 5), Danish competitiveness measured in terms of relative unit labour costs in manufacturing improved considerably at the beginning of the decade, but deteriorated in the 1986-87 boom years. In the following years of competitive disinflation, relative wage increases slowed and overall relative unit labour costs improved somewhat despite a small setback in 1989-90. The devaluations in the second half of 1992 led to a deterioration of competitiveness *vis-à-vis* particularly Sweden and the UK. However, in overall terms the devaluations only meant a return to the level of competitiveness of 1990. Labour costs per hour are not out of line with the main trading partners (see Table 6).

Table 6

Labour costs per hour in manufacturing

(DKR)

	1991
Belgium	125
Denmark	116
Finland	133
France	98
Germany	142
Italy	110
Netherlands	119
Norway	142
Spain	81
Sweden	142
United Kingdom	86

Source: Swedish Employer Confederation: wages and total labour centre for workers.

Furthermore, the development in productivity does not give cause for concern. Productivity continued to increase in the 1980s. Overall labour productivity of the Danish economy grew at an annual rate of 1,7% over the decade. This was slightly below the Community average of 1,9% on average

per year over the decade, but Denmark has not experienced a lower productivity growth in comparison with other similar countries in the period 1973-89.

In total manufacturing, labour productivity increased by 0,5% per year over the decade (see Graph 20). The increase can particularly be ascribed to the food, beverages and tobacco industries where labour productivity increased by 3,8% per year. This is partly due to the concentration on larger units in these sectors in the period. In industries like metal fabricated products and paper, printing and publishing, productivity seems to have declined in the 1980s. The phenomenon of productivity decreasing in manufacturing in a period of relatively high investment in new technologies is somewhat peculiar and has attracted some attention. It has been found that there was a concentration of investment in new technology in the years 1983-86 across all industries. The introduction of new technology is not always easy, and in the Danish case it led to a period of higher employment due to the introduction of new technology. This also means that prospects are for higher productivity increases in the manufacturing industry as has also been witnessed at the beginning of the 1990s.

In market services, labour productivity increased by 2% per year over the decade. Structural changes, like concentration on larger units (e.g. supermarkets and banks), as well as increased computerization should enable many service sectors to continue to increase labour productivity. Productivity increases in education, for example, may be much harder to achieve, and they do not seem to have materialized, but the whole question of measuring productivity in service industries is often very difficult.

Prospects point towards higher Danish productivity increases, and the overall productivity developments in the 1980s, therefore, do not give cause for concern. Considering the development in labour costs as well as productivity, in overall terms Danish firms do not currently seem to be at a cost disadvantage. On the other hand, the Danish cost level when making an international comparison is still very high, and this may cause problems in particularly sensitive industries. Further rationalization and automation are not always enough to ensure productivity in a country in particularly exposed industries.

3.2.2. The size structure of Danish industrial companies

Danish industry consists mainly of small to medium-sized companies by international standards. In a recent study, the Danish Ministry of Finance (*Finansredegørelse 92*) found

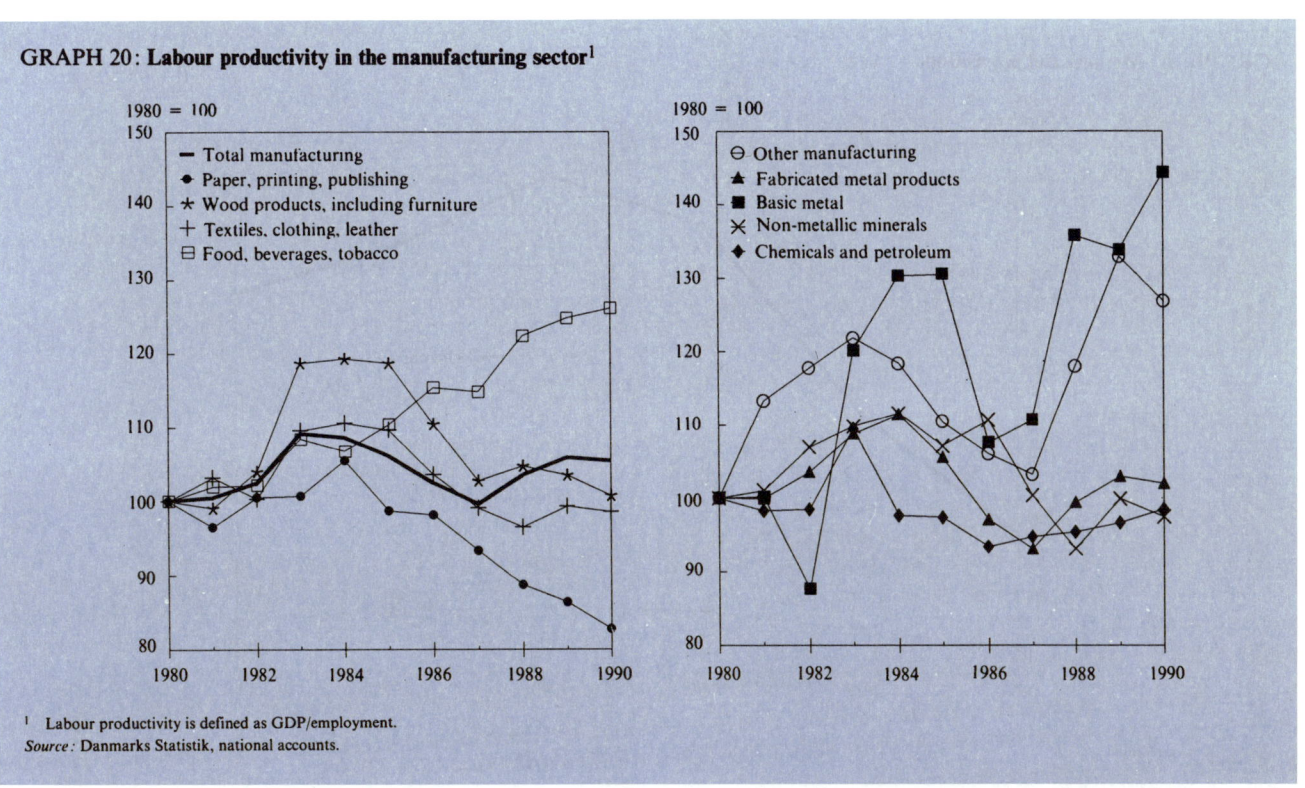

GRAPH 20: **Labour productivity in the manufacturing sector**[1]

1980 = 100

- Total manufacturing
- Paper, printing, publishing
- Wood products, including furniture
- Textiles, clothing, leather
- Food, beverages, tobacco

1980 = 100

- Other manufacturing
- Fabricated metal products
- Basic metal
- Non-metallic minerals
- Chemicals and petroleum

[1] Labour productivity is defined as GDP/employment.
Source: Danmarks Statistik, national accounts.

30 corporations in the services, construction and manufacturing sectors with a turnover of more than DKR 2,5 billion, a turnover abroad of at least DKR 1 billion, and more than 2 000 employees. However, the biggest manufacturing corporation is the brewing group Carlsberg with about 14 000 employees. There are no multinational companies of a size comparable to Philips, Alcatel or Daimler-Benz.

Big companies are often thought to have a critical role in the growth process, because they are believed to be able to act as 'industrial locomotives', meaning that big companies normally attract a cluster of sub-suppliers and therefore have a bigger effect on employment than simply their own number of employees. The creation of one job in the biggest Danish manufacturing corporations has thus been calculated to create 1,9 jobs in other Danish companies, and for the biggest service corporations the figure is 1,4.

Following this logic, the size structure of Danish industry with its lack of large companies could be argued to be a major disadvantage in the European internal market. Indeed, the Cecchini report argues that the biggest effects of the

internal market stem from increasing the size of enterprises. Therefore, the size structure of Danish industry could potentially act as a barrier to growth and increasing employment. An increase in the number of M&As would, on the other hand, be an indication that Danish industry has prepared itself for the internal market. The internal market should in particular have led to an increase in the number of horizontal M&As, because of the possibility of improving economies of scale.

Graph 21 shows that this was indeed the case. In the period 1987-92, the number of M&As increased from about 100 to about 300 to 350 per year in 1989 and 1991. As expected, the level of horizontal M&As in particular seems to have increased. The level of horizontal M&As was about 100 in the period 1983-87. Assuming this to be the 'normal' level an accumulated number of 'above normal' horizontal M&As of about 850 took place in the period 1987-92. The number of diversifications also saw an increase in 1988 and 1989. However, the increase was not as dramatic as for the horizontal M&As, and there may have been a good deal of the 'me too' effect in this.

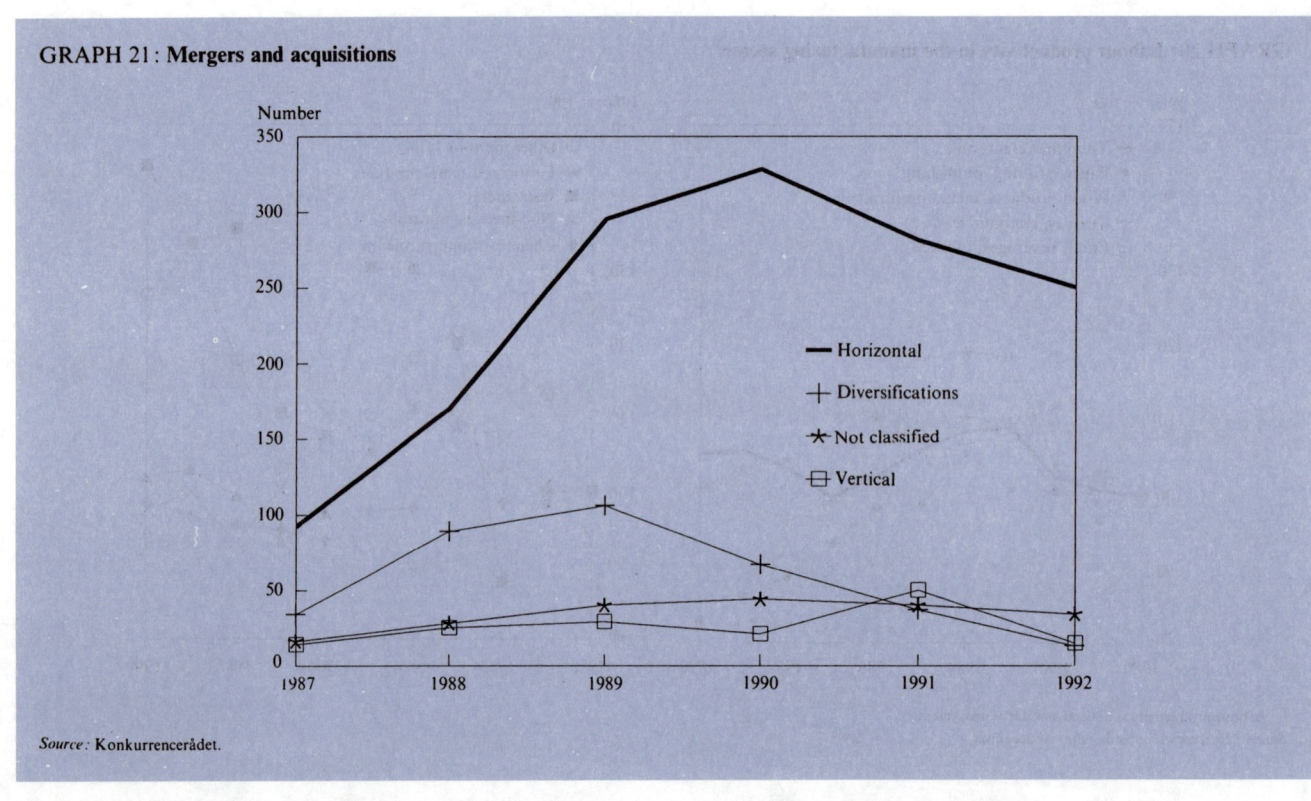

GRAPH 21 : Mergers and acquisitions

Number

- Horizontal
- + Diversifications
- * Not classified
- Vertical

Source : Konkurrencerådet.

Obviously, the bigger an M&A, the bigger the impact on the economy is likely to be. However, many of the additional M&As in the period 1987-92 took place between smaller companies. In 1991 the acquired or merged companies on average had only 76 employees, and only seven had more than 500 employees. The EC Commission collects data on M&As between the 1 000 largest European manufacturing companies, the 500 largest companies world-wide as well as the largest services companies. The statistics provide figures on M&As where the combined turnover is more than ECU 1 billion. In Denmark, the development in the number of such large M&As basically shows the same picture as the total number of M&As. Table 7 shows that in 1988/89 two Danish companies out of a total of 492 EC companies took part in such big M&As. In 1989/90 it jumped to 16 out of 622 and in 1990/91 to 14 out of 455. In 1990/91, only two companies were acquired by other Danish companies in a big merger. Five of the companies went to other EC companies, four to Swedish companies and three to Norwegian companies. It should be noted that in these statistics some of the big M&As in recent years involving Danish companies took place between financial companies.

The impact of the additional M&As at the end of the 1980s and beginning of the 1990s on the structure of Danish

industry is not easy to evaluate, but from a global point of view it has not meant a significant change in the overall size structure. The M&As involved only about 2% of the employees in the manufacturing, construction and services sectors (excluding financial services) in each of the years 1987 to 1989. About 50% of the M&As took place in manufacturing, and the M&As affected between 3 and 7% of employees in manufacturing in each of the years 1987 to 1992. However, these figures for manufacturing are strongly influenced by a few big M&As in the food products industry. By international standards the Danish industry structure is still dominated by small to medium-sized enterprises.

Nevertheless, there is no doubt that the M&As have led to adaptations which were important as a preparation for the internal market. The concentration has increased on strategically important points in the industrial system, and groups which can better exploit their particular opportunities have been created. This has been the case, for example, in the food products industry. A few cases illustrate the process:

(i) In 1989 the corporation Danisco was created in a merger between De Danske Spritfabrikker (Danish distillers), De Danske Sukkerfabrikker (Danish sugar), and Danisco. Danisco produces a broad range of food products

Table 7

Majority acquisitions (including mergers) by Member State[1]

	1986/87	1987/88	1988/89	1989/90	1990/91	1991/92
Belgium	3	11	18	21	9	5
Denmark	1	2	2	16	14	3
Germany	69	51	90	124	111	155
Greece	—	—	—	3	8	3
Spain	20	27	65	74	35	18
France	63	122	112	101	115	64
Ireland	2	6	8	3	2	5
Italy	35	40	49	73	51	38
Luxembourg	1	—	4	3	—	—
Netherlands	19	16	23	28	21	11
Portugal	—	2	10	8	7	1
United Kingdom	90	106	111	168	82	44
Total	303	383	492	622	455	347

[1] Figures are from the period June to May.

Source: Commission services.

including liquor, sugar, frozen foods and ice-cream, but also owns packaging and paper factories, engineering firms, machinery factories, etc.

(ii) The Danish dairy industry had 524 firms in 1970. Today the industry consists of one dominant, one medium-sized and a few smaller firms. The dominant firm is MD-Foods which has been created over the years through a number of M&As. MD-Foods processes two thirds of all milk produced in Denmark and accounts for 90% of the Danish export of dairy products.

(iii) The slaughtering industry today, like the dairy industry, is a highly concentrated industry, where the companies have been formed through a series of mergers. A merger in 1990 between three slaughtering firms created the company 'Danish Crown', which processes more than 7,5 million pigs per year and is the largest slaughtering firm in Europe.

These M&As did not take place only as a preparation for the internal market. The concentration in the dairy and slaughtering industries has been an on-going process for many years. However, M&As have increased Danish competitiveness by strengthening key competitive positions in the industrial system, and as such are good examples of how competitiveness can be strengthened in the face of the internal market. They also illustrate that the kind of mega-mergers needed to create a few big companies by inter-national standards might not even have been desirable given the Danish industry structure. Bigger M&As than those seen might have been damaging to the Danish economy, because too big an M&A can paralyse a company for a long time.

The biggest companies are the backbone of the Danish industry structure, and they undoubtedly play an essential role in the Danish economy. On the other hand, one of the key aspects of the internal market is the opportunity for smaller firms to internationalize and possibly become sub-contractors to big foreign corporations. The introduction of 'lean production' methods in big companies and the accompanying sourcing-out of non-core functions will tend to reinforce this trend. Therefore, in a discussion of company size it should be considered that companies need to have an optimal size for the strategies they are pursuing. Therefore the size structure as such does not have to be a major disadvantage for Denmark in the internal market.

3.2.3. The internationalization of Danish industry

Danish industry is highly internationalized. Exports of goods and services amount to 35% of GDP. The Community accounted for 54% and the EFTA countries for 23% of Danish exports of goods in 1992. Services amount to about 22% of the total export of goods, and tourism and shipping account for about two thirds of the Danish export of services.

The share of services in total exports has been largely constant throughout the 1980s, and as a percentage of GDP it increased from 7,1 to 7,8% between 1980 and 1990. However, it is commonly acknowledged that service industries will become more international, and exports of services should increase their relative importance in the future. The internal market will contribute to this development.

The product groups dominating Danish exports of goods have not changed during the 1980s. As seen from Table 9, food products are still the single most important export group, but the weight has shifted towards manufactured goods. The increase in the share of fuels in total exports is a consequence of increased Danish production of North Sea oil and gas. It should also be noted that not even agricultural products have experienced a decline in absolute terms, since Danish exports have seen a sharp increase between 1981 and 1992 — particularly after 1990 due to German unification. As seen from Table 8, the dominant markets have not changed either between 1981 and 1992. The biggest markets continued to be Germany, Sweden and the United Kingdom, with about 77% of total exports going to EC and EFTA countries. However, some important changes have taken place. Unified Germany is the absolutely dominant export market, and, partly as a consequence of German unification, the EC share has increased to 54%.

Table 8

Share of Danish exports of main trading partners

		(%)
	1981	1992
EC	47,4	54,0
EFTA	23,7	22,8
France	4,8	5,8
Germany	16,7	22,4
Italy	4,6	4,9
Japan	2,9	3,6
Norway	6,2	5,5
Sweden	11,5	11,5
UK	13,6	10,3
USA	5,3	4,6

Source: Danmarks Statistik.

The geographical distribution of Danish exports reflects the fact that Danish companies have in their internationalization process often tended to start exporting to countries like Sweden, Germany and the United Kingdom, countries culturally similar to Denmark, before moving to the rest of

Table 9

The most important Danish export articles

		(%)
	1981	1992
Food products	30,9	25,6
Raw materials	7,8	4,9
Fuels	3,3	4,0
Chemicals	7,8	10,0
of which: Pharmaceuticals	2,3	3,9
Semi-manufactured products	12,2	11,2
Machines and transport equipment	24,6	26,9
Other manufactured goods	13,5	17,4
of which: Furniture	2,9	4,2
Clothing	2,3	3,0
Measuring instruments	1,9	2,3
Total	100,0	100,0

Source: Danmarks Statistik.

the world. However, the geographical coverage of Danish exports is very high even for quite small companies. Using a random sample of manufacturing companies with foreign sales, Schultz, Strandskov and Vestergaard (1986) found that the biggest manufacturing companies with more than 500 employees had on average 33 export markets in 1986 (see Graph 22). As would be expected, the number of export markets increased with the size of the company, but even very small companies appear to have quite widespread export activities. On the other hand, in another context it has been estimated that 10% of firms account for 60% of total exports. The major part of Danish exports is therefore carried out by relatively few firms.

The establishment of the internal market will facilitate trade, and particularly the internationalization of small to medium-sized firms. In order to be able to profit from the opportunities offered by the internal market, a strengthening of the international market position of Danish companies will be very important. Danish foreign direct investment flows indicate that such a process has taken place. Graph 23 shows that Danish foreign direct investments more than doubled as a percentage of GDP in the period 1987-91.

Graph 23 also shows that foreign direct investment flows to Denmark increased dramatically in the period 1987-91, possibly indicating a further specialization of Danish industry. The biggest foreign investors were the Community and the other Scandinavian countries. Sweden particularly was

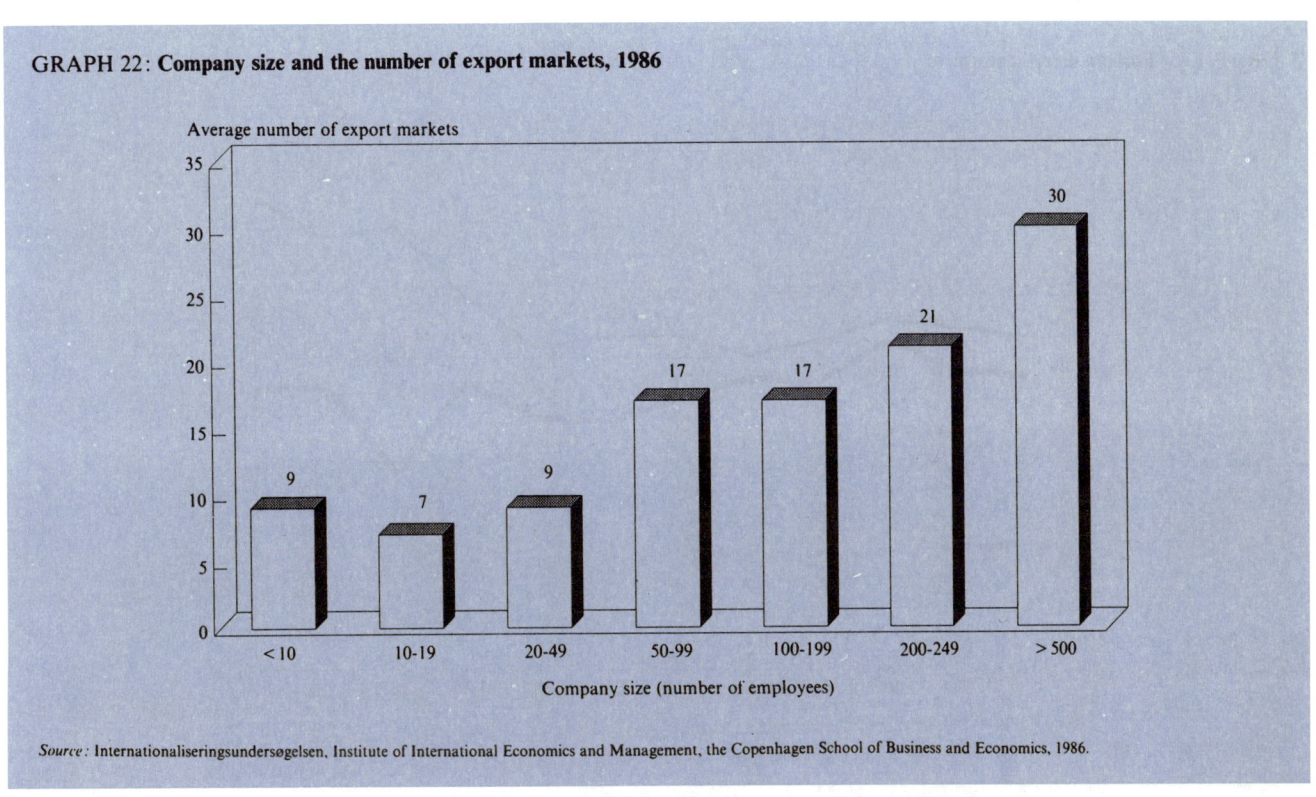

GRAPH 22: **Company size and the number of export markets, 1986**

Average number of export markets

Company size (number of employees)

Source: Internationaliseringsundersøgelsen, Institute of International Economics and Management, the Copenhagen School of Business and Economics, 1986.

a big investor in Denmark. However, the Swedish figures are influenced by the fact that SAS's investment in Denmark is registered as Swedish foreign direct investment, but some Swedish firms probably also wanted to establish a bridgehead in the Community. American companies on the other hand have not been as big investors in the 1980s as they were earlier. The biggest areas for foreign direct investment in Denmark have been manufacturing, transport, trade and finance, but, as mentioned above, transport is to a large extent influenced by SAS's investment in Denmark.

The surge in foreign direct investment in the period 1987-91 has been experienced by all EC countries. This consolidation of international market positions was to be expected as a preparation for the internal market. In the Danish case the preparations for the internal market were less dramatic than might have been expected, because Danish firms had already internationalized before 1986. Therefore, in overall terms, this process does not give rise to concern. The companies which have been primarily domestically oriented, for example those that focused on public sector contracts, have faced or will face the greatest need for restructuring. Some of these companies have already had to reduce their level of

employment or have even gone out of business, but those restructurings were necessary, and probably of a relatively smaller magnitude than in many other EC countries.

3.2.4. Conclusion: the competitive position of Danish industry

The recent revaluation of the Danish krone may have led to short-term competitiveness problems, but Danish industry does not seem to have an unfavourable cost position, even though the high Danish cost level can be a problem in particularly sensitive industries. Furthermore, it cannot be concluded that size structure is a disadvantage and that the Danish economy needs M&As which could create a few big corporations by international standards, in order to be competitive in the internal market. Such big M&As may even be damaging, because they can paralyse companies for a long period of time. It is also positive that Danish companies seem to have strengthened their international market position as a preparation for the internal market. Danish industry was already highly internationalized before the project for the European internal market took shape. This was

45

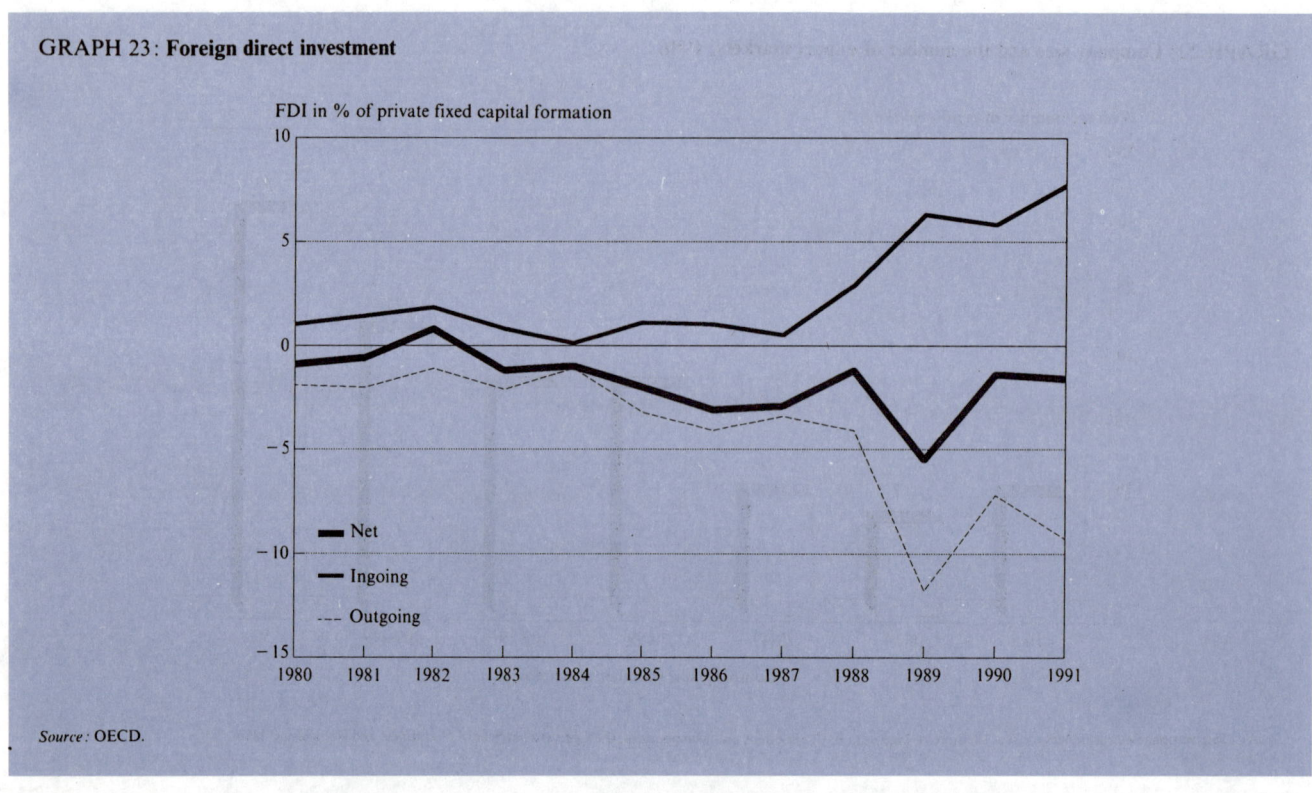

GRAPH 23: **Foreign direct investment**

FDI in % of private fixed capital formation

Net
Ingoing
Outgoing

Source: OECD.

the case even for quite small companies, and the further internationalization, as a preparation for the internal market, was therefore less dramatic than might have been expected.

Overall, the competitive position of Danish industry in the integrating European economy seems to be quite strong. However, this does not necessarily mean that growth and employment-creation prospects are favourable, as will be discussed in Section 3.

3.3. Industrial development prospects

3.3.1. The specialization of Danish industry

Danish industrial structure is very diversified, but its strength lies in mature low-growth, often low-tech, areas like food products, furniture and shipbuilding. Denmark has a strong position in pharmaceuticals, which is a high-growth area, but in general its presence in what are often called the 'industries of the future' is rather limited. The 'built-in'

growth rate of Danish industry therefore seems limited, simply due to the composition of the industrial sector.

However, this kind of analysis is by necessity somewhat superficial. There may be opportunities to develop some high-tech niche industries, and the growth prospects of mature Danish industries may be quite different from the European or global average. Furthermore, some of the service industries may have very good growth opportunities. A more detailed analysis, focusing on the fundamentals of individual industries, is necessary in order to understand the growth prospects of the Danish economy. In the appendix to this chapter the developments in the Danish dairy, slaughtering, textiles, pharmaceuticals, sea-transport, shipbuilding and business service industries are discussed in order to analyse the situation. These are key industries in the Danish economy.

The important food-products industry illustrates the dynamics and the problems in evaluating the growth prospects of a mature industry. The integrating European economy has led to development towards a higher concentration on the retail as well as the producer side. This could cause, for example, the Danish dairy and slaughtering companies (which in this context are only medium-sized) to be squeezed, and they may be forced to adopt their strategies and to a larger extent become sub-suppliers to big multinational food corporations. The effect of such a change on growth, employment and exports is extremely difficult to evaluate. On the one hand, it is a further specialization, which would tend to reduce employment. On the other hand, it could also provide access to new markets. Furthermore, new food-products segments are developing in prepared foods, and this will create new opportunities and scope for business development in the food-products industry.

It is difficult to provide a qualitative assessment of the growth prospects of a high-growth industry like pharmaceuticals. Danish producers have strong positions in insulin, antibiotics, vitamins, diuretics, sulphonamides and psycho-pharmaceuticals. Research and development is a key to survival and growth in the industry, with related expenses often of the magnitude of 10 to 20% of a company's turnover. In some studies it has been found that Danish pharmaceutical companies spend less on research and development than other pharmaceutical companies. This could indicate a potential competitive weakness and slower growth prospects. The size of Danish companies in this industry may be a disadvantage and could lead to further strategic alliances with foreign companies. Such a development would not necessarily be a disadvantage for the Danish economy.

A high-growth industry like pharmaceuticals normally has a higher growth potential than mature industries. However, industries like food products, textiles and clothing, ship-building and sea transport have been able to prosper through innovation and entrepreneurship, even though they can hardly be considered as the 'industries of the future'. Business development and growth is possible in mature industries, but will depend on the competitiveness of the companies in a given industry.

The outlook for manufacturing is quite favourable, but employment-creation opportunities are probably better in the service industries. Some service industries, like retailing and to a certain extent transportation, are mature industries, but long-term trends will cause growth in several service industries. Increasing real incomes and leisure time will for example increase the demand for leisure-time services like travel services, sports facilities, cultural activities, etc., and the higher proportion of elderly people will lead to a greater demand for health services. Furthermore, in the 1980s, firms have tended to concentrate on their core activities and externalize marginal functions. This trend is, firstly, a consequence of firms finding that it is a more cost-efficient way of operating ('lean production'), and secondly, it often provides more flexibility in an environment, where the ability to respond fast becomes more and more important. This development will in turn create jobs in the business services sector. Another important trend comes from the diffusion of information technology, which will lead to the development of new information services products.

The Danish Government has pointed out that the potential for job creation lies in the services sectors and particularly in increased demand for household services through a reduction of 'do-it-yourself' work and the black economy. The high marginal tax rate as well as the high minimum salary is believed to have caused a higher than optimal rate of 'do-it-yourself' work and a proliferation of the black economy. Nowadays, it is simply too expensive for a household to have cleaning assistance for example, because the service is quite expensive due to high minimum salaries and must be paid for from income which has been taxed at 68%. Obviously the potential for moonlighting is quite high in this area. It is probably also the case that some people draw benefits from the rather generous unemployment benefit system (see Section 2 in Chapters 1 and 2), while working at the same time in the black economy.

It would seem important to remedy this situation, and from an overall point of view several service areas will clearly be among the high-growth areas of the future. However, manufacturing will continue to be an important sector in the Danish economy. It is particularly important in this connection to recognize the often very complex interrelationships between manufacturing and the services sectors. This is illustrated in the case of the Danish shipbuilding and sea transport industries, where both industries are dependent on each other for their future development. The same type of interdependence can be found between other industries as well, for example pharmaceuticals and the health sector. In many cases, therefore, it is not possible simply to carry out the discussion in terms of 'manufacturing' and 'services' industries. There may be potential for business development and creation of high-productivity jobs in improved interrelationships between services and manufacturing industries. Public sector services will also have an important role to play in this respect.

3.3.2. Technological innovation, and research and development

The discussion in Section 3.1 naturally raises the question of increasing the emphasis on so-called 'high-tech/high-growth' industries of the future. Furthermore, it has also been found that in trade between industrialized countries technological innovation is a more important factor for competitiveness than cost. Research and development (R&D) are without doubt highly important for competitiveness and the industrial development prospects of a country.

The most common indicator in comparisons of R&D activities in different countries is the level of R&D expenditure as a percentage of GDP. In Graph 24 and Table 10 it is seen that, during the last 10 years, Denmark has increased its expenditure on R&D (as a percentage of GDP) significantly, compared to EUR 12 and Germany. However, Denmark still spends less than the EC average in terms of ecus per capita and only a little more than half of German expenditure per capita. It is also seen from Table 10 that Denmark is below the EC average and is lagging behind Germany with regard to the number of R&D personnel per thousand of the labour force. Furthermore, in Denmark the government finances a bigger share while Danish industry finances a significantly smaller share of R&D than its German counterparts and the EC average. The relatively low R&D activity in Danish industry is to a large extent due to the absence of large multinational corporations as well as the predominance of less research-intensive mature industries.

There are some statistical problems with comparisons based on R&D expenditure as a percentage of GDP, because this indicator is basically an input measure. In Table 10, the inventiveness coefficient (the number of patents per 10 000

inhabitants), is shown. Measured on this indicator, Denmark has a higher innovative activity than the Community as a whole, but only half that of Germany. However, this measure also has some serious limitations, because patents only cover

Table 10

Research and development indicators

	Denmark	EUR 12	Germany
GERD in ecus per capita (1990)[1]	289,4	297,9	530,0
Total R&D personnel per thousand labour force	8,5	9,3	14,3
Percentage of GERD financed by industry (1989)	46,8	52,9	63,3
Percentage of GERD financed by government (1989)	45,5	40,7	34,1
Inventiveness coefficient[2]	2,5	2,2	4,9

[1] GERD = gross domestic expenditure on R&D.
[2] Inventiveness coefficient = domestic patent applications per 10 000 inhabitants (1990).
Source: Eurostat: *Government financing of research and development, 1992,* and OECD: *Main science and technology indicators, 1992.*

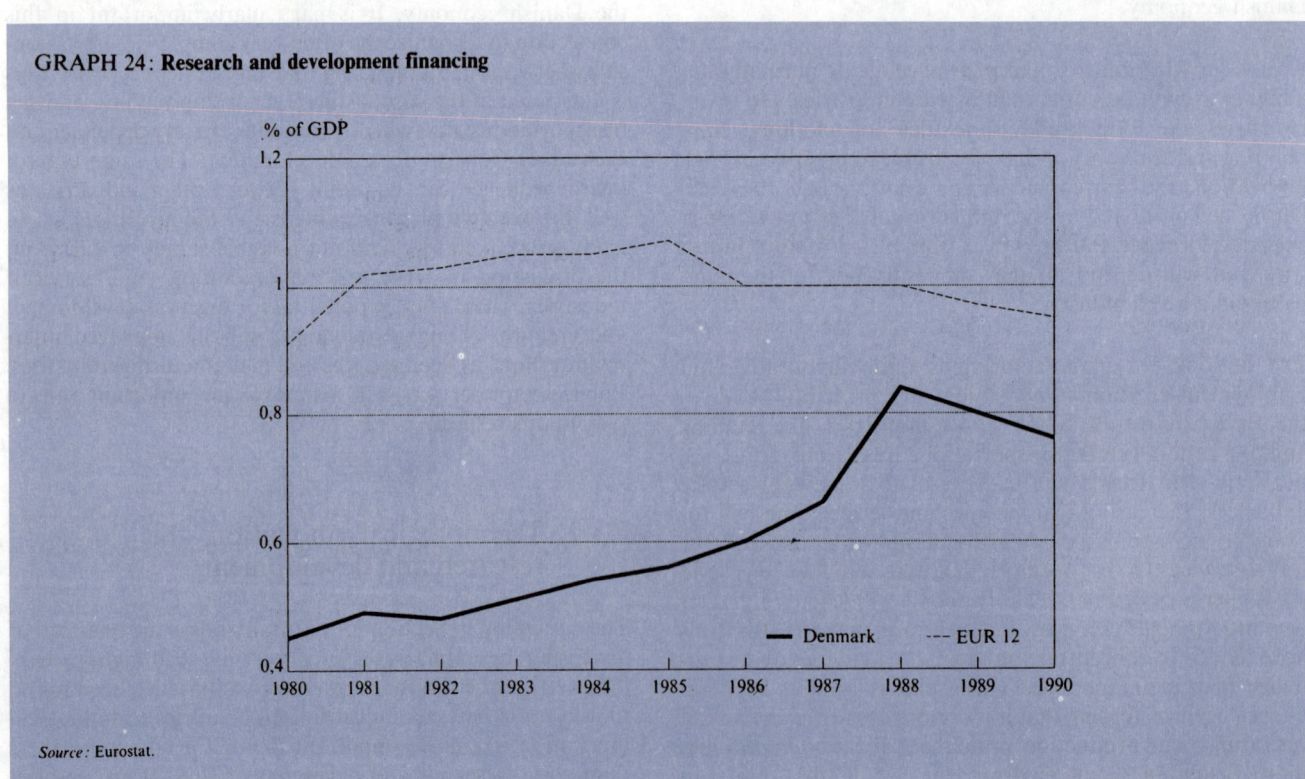

GRAPH 24: **Research and development financing**

% of GDP

Denmark   --- EUR 12

Source: Eurostat.

a part of all innovations. This is due firstly to the fact that taking out a patent makes detailed information about an innovation publicly available to potential competitors. Secondly, the technological development is so rapid in many areas that it simply does not pay to patent new inventions.

In general, Denmark seems to devote relatively few resources to R&D — an increased allocation of resources to R&D would probably lead to an improved competitive position, but in a small country the way in which R&D resources are spent and the ability to adopt new technology is more important than the absolute level of resources allocated. Participating in the main stream of research-intensive high-tech industries requires enormous amounts of resources. It may not be possible for a small country to commit the resources necessary to become a major player in one or more of these high-tech industries. A company like IBM spends more on R&D than countries like Australia, Belgium and Denmark. The presence of large multinational corporations in an economy may make it possible to overcome such barriers. This has been the case in Sweden, Switzerland and the Netherlands. However, given the size structure of Danish industrial firms, participation in main-stream high-tech industries would seem possible only through participation in international joint R&D projects, for example those sponsored by the Community. Therefore, viewed from a Danish perspective, it would appear less worthwhile simply to try to boost high-tech industries through an increased allocation of R&D resources. Instead, provision of know-how in technological progress should be given high priority in order to improve product development and production processes.

In the future, Danish R&D efforts should take as a starting point the sectors where Danish companies are competitive. An interesting new R&D programme, which points in this direction, has been established in food technology. The programme is the first to be administered in cooperation with several ministries, and one aim is to strengthen Danish competitiveness through the promotion of cooperation between existing research institutions and private enterprises. In this way the programme should contribute to a better exchange of knowledge and an improved coordination of research activities in food technology leading to an increase in the know-how content of food technology. There have, however, been some initial difficulties in the administration of the programme. Other new measures to bolster R&D include a newly created fund supporting basic research and reduced taxation of foreign researchers working in Denmark.

The Danish level of R&D is relatively low by international standards, but innovation performance is not determined by a single factor. There is a strong interdependence between innovation, R&D, infrastructure, marketing, education, training, entrepreneurship, etc. In this respect the fundamental conditions for R&D and innovation in Denmark are good. The infrastructure and the general level of education in the work-force are among the best by international standards and a few large companies carry out international R&D while many innovative small and medium-sized firms have the potential to compete on an international basis. There is no reason why Denmark should not be able to prosper even in some high-tech niche areas. It should also be noted that it is unlikely that the innovation performance of a country can be increased rapidly through a rise in public expenditure devoted to R&D. Innovation is a complex, long-term process involving many factors, of which only some can be provided by government.

3.3.3. Industry structure, new company formation and employment

As already mentioned, Denmark has its strongest competitive positions in relatively mature industries. However, many of the larger Danish companies have achieved dominant positions on the home market in the same industries. This is, for example, the case in food-products industries like brewing, slaughtering and dairy products, which are highly concentrated.

The dominant position on the home market has been a good platform for the internationalization process of these companies, making many of them large exporters. However, it also means that the prospects for job creation in general may be better in the small to medium-sized businesses than in the large companies, since the concentration process which created many of the large companies also led to rationalization and restructuring of the industries they now dominate. Furthermore, the progress in factory and office automation techniques as well as the trend towards 'leaner' production methods mean that the rationalization process will continue. Employment-creation prospects seem better in small to medium-sized enterprises.

On an overall level, new companies made up about 5% of the total number of companies in 1989, corresponding to 15 000 new companies per year, creating employment for about 25 000 persons in the first year of establishment. This is relatively low in comparison with other countries. However, the structure of Danish industry should also be considered in this connection. Mature, highly concentrated industries are, for example, not an easy environment in which to start a new company. It is much easier in a fragmented industry like textiles, where economies of scale are of less importance. In comparing start-up rates between

Table 11

Regional distribution of employment

(%)

	Employment 1980			Employment 1988		
	Copenhagen	The islands	Jutland	Copenhagen	The islands	Jutland
Agriculture	5,8	26,7	67,5	6,0	26,9	67,1
Manufacturing, mining and utilities	30,3	20,7	49,0	28,9	12,8	58,3
Construction	28,9	22,9	48,2	30,1	22,8	47,1
Private services	41,3	17,6	41,1	41,7	17,3	41,0
Public services	41,3	18,7	40,0	37,9	19,5	42,6
Other	30,5	19,3	50,2	31,2	21,1	47,7
Total	35,6	19,6	44,7	34,7	19,4	45,9

Source: Registerbaserede Beskaftigelsesstatistik, *Statistiks Årbog*, Danmarks Statistik.

countries, differences in industry structures must also be considered.

A considerable amount of entrepreneurial dynamics is witnessed in regional changes which have taken place over the last 20 years. Manufacturing industries have tended to move out of the bigger cities. Copenhagen is by far the largest city, so a move of manufacturing industries to the western part of Denmark is involved. Employment in the services industries has, on the other hand, increased in the Copenhagen area (see Table 11). Maskell (1992) found that this process was due both to a higher rate of company closures in the bigger cities as well as a higher rate of new company establishments in the smaller cities. At the same time, the size structure of manufacturing remained more or less stable in the period 1972-88, and the biggest and oldest companies persisted. That is, the changes mainly took place at the level of small to medium-sized companies. It is also noteworthy that the overall structure seems to be largely unchanged, which means that the turnover of companies tended to take place within the same industries. In any case, the regional dynamics show that new company formation is possible even in mature manufacturing industries.

However, it would seem necessary to promote and support entrepreneurship in order to increase job creation and growth even though a considerable amount of entrepreneurial dynamics is already present. A network of technological service centres exists in order to support small to medium-sized business. Due to the predominance in the industry structure of small to medium-sized businesses it would seem absolutely essential to secure a high level of technology utilization and a high degree of professionalization in the small to medium-sized business sector. From a strategic point of view it would seem important for small to medium-sized Danish companies to become even more international and specialized in order to respond to the needs and opportunities of the internal market. Support will be necessary in order to overcome the difficulties of internationalization. The encouragement of entrepreneurship is included in the most recent government measures, and the Danish Government has established a 'network programme' to further cooperation between small to medium-sized companies, but it is still too early to evaluate the effect of the programme.

3.3.4. Regionalization and economic development

In the Cecchini report, the internal market was estimated to provide a boost to growth and employment in the Community. However, the question is how it will affect the individual regions in the Community and particularly how the benefits of the internal market will be distributed between regions. In this context, Denmark can be considered by and large as one region.

From an economic point of view, the internal market programme basically aims at reducing trading costs. This would in itself tend to favour location of production in the peripheral regions due to their generally lower labour costs. On the other hand, it will also make it more profitable to concentrate production on fewer locations, i.e. the market will become less fragmented and production more polarized.

Particular industries have often clustered in particular regions thereby forming industrial complexes, and it is often an advantage for a firm to locate in a region with a cluster of similar companies because of, for example, a suitable infrastructure and a labour force with the right qualifications. Therefore, the internal market programme could easily lead to a strengthening of existing developed core regions in the Community and potentially to a weakening of the peripheral regions. In this context South-East England, the Benelux, southern and western Germany, north-eastern France and northern Italy, as well as the Barcelona and Madrid regions, are often considered to be the core and the rest of the Community the periphery. The aim of the Community Structural Funds is precisely to increase the convergence between the regions.

In the case of Denmark, the question is to what extent the location at the periphery of the Community will be a disadvantage for economic development in the integrating European economy. The Danish position cannot be compared with the situation of other peripheral regions in the Community, since Denmark is not a low-wage country. However, Denmark has very close ties with the rest of Scandinavia and the developments in Eastern Europe should also lead to the re-establishment of pre-World-War-II trade links. Economically therefore, Denmark is not seen as a peripheral country in Europe, but could in fact be an attractive place for new investment.

Studies have shown that foreign direct investment in Denmark to a large extent is focused on the Danish home market. In the future it would seem desirable to attract investments aimed at using Denmark as an export base. Therefore, from the perspective of localization and polarization, it would seem necessary to improve the infrastructure in order to avoid marginalization and to exploit the favourable location between Scandinavia, the Baltic countries, and the rest of the Community. From this perspective it would also seem advisable to strengthen existing industrial complexes in order to create environments attractive for foreign investors. R&D as well as education will, seen from this perspective, also play a key role.

3.4. The May 1993 measures for furthering industrial development

A wide range of general measures such as changes in the tax system and labour-market structures, as discussed in Sections 1.2.5 and 1.3.4 of Chapter 1, have the potential to influence industrial development. However, the recent fiscal package also included some more specific measures.

The efforts to provide guidance and education of entrepreneurs will be strengthened, and the subsidies allocated to testing and developing the product ideas of entrepreneurs will be increased. Furthermore, the existing research programme in food technology will be strengthened.

As mentioned in Section 3.1, Denmark seems to have a relatively low consumption of household services, and there appears to be a potential for job creation in this area through a reduction of 'do-it-yourself activities' and moonlighting. The government will therefore introduce a new scheme through which private companies providing household services like cleaning, cooking and gardening can receive wage subsidies. The programme is in particular expected to create jobs for unskilled labour.

In addition, a number of infrastructure investments have been moved forward: roads for example. However, a number of big infrastructure investments are already being undertaken or are planned in Denmark. Huge investments are being made in the railways, as well as in spectacular new projects like the tunnel/bridge across the Great Belt between Jutland and Funen as well as the tunnel/bridge across the Øresund between Sweden and Denmark.

3.5. Conclusions

The overall competitive position of Danish industry in the integrating European economy is quite good; on average the cost competitiveness is good despite the recent devaluations, and the wave of mergers and acquisitions at the end of the 1980s and beginning of the 1990s has led to a strengthening of Danish key competitive positions and Danish companies have internationalized further as a preparation for the internal market.

However, prospects for growth and employment creation in the manufacturing sector are mixed. At first glance, a manufacturing industry consisting of small to medium-sized companies in predominantly mature industries seems to be a very unfavourable structure, but the Danish prospects in many of the more mature industries are quite good, and this leaves room for optimism.

The level of Danish R&D is relatively low compared with other industrialized countries, but it cannot be concluded that more resources must be allocated to R&D related to high-tech/high-growth industries. In a small country, the way in which the resources are utilized is more important than the absolute level. It would seem advisable to focus on R&D relevant to industries where strong competitive positions have already been achieved.

New company formation and business development in the small to medium-sized business sector will probably be the main source of new jobs in the manufacturing industries. Scope for expansion in the larger companies in highly concentrated industries seems limited, at least in their activities in Denmark. The services industries are likely to be major providers of new jobs in the future. This is partly a consequence of some general trends, such as the diffusion of information technology, the increase in real incomes and leisure time, the increased sophistication of business as well as the tendency for companies to externalize more non-core functions. Furthermore, the Danish Ministry of Finance has argued that there might a potential for new jobs in household services, if the black economy and 'do-it-yourself' work could be reduced. The black economy seems to have proliferated in this area, and the amount of 'do-it-yourself' work is relatively high, due to high marginal taxes.

However, when considering the employment and growth prospects of manufacturing and services industries, the interrelationships between them should also be considered. Business development prospects both in Danish manufacturing and services industries may to a large extent depend on the ability to exploit and improve such interrelationships.

The internal market will be an opportunity for Denmark to overcome the abovementioned disadvantages of the industry structure, because business will increasingly have a more European or even global perspective. A main economic policy issue will be to attract investment and promote industrial development. Given the current position of Danish industry the prospects should in this respect be quite good. However, it would seem essential to continue to improve the structural workings of the economy, for example the labour market, the educational system, the tax system and the infrastructure, thereby improving the framework for entrepreneurial activities.

Appendix

Food products: the dairy and slaughtering industries

The Danish food-products industry is made up of a number of quite different food-products industries. The biggest industries in the food-products industry are the slaughtering, dairy, fishing-products, baking and brewing industries (see Table 12). The competitive situation is quite different in the various food-products industries. The slaughtering, dairy and brewing industries are heavily concentrated. The fishing-products and baking industries are not to the same extent concentrated. The food-products industries are all very international, with high export shares. The following section will focus on the dairy and slaughtering industries. They are the two biggest industries and can be discussed together, because their structures are quite similar.

The concentration of the dairy and slaughtering industries has led to the creation of internationally competitive firms, which have been able to build up strong international market positions. The competitive situation will become more difficult in the internal market, and the need to possess international brands may mean that these industries could be faced with very tough strategic decisions, for example, whether to create their own brands and therefore compete directly with bigger multinational food corporations, or whether they should accept a role as subcontractors to these bigger multinational corporations. Concentration is taking place at a European level not only among the companies in the food-products industry, but also on the retail side. Both trends may mean that the medium-sized (in this context) Danish dairy and slaughtering corporations could get squeezed if they choose to compete directly with the large multinational food-products corporations.

Another weak point is the relatively lower R&D activity of the companies in the Danish food-products industry sector. It has been estimated that the companies in this sector spend only about 1% of their sales on R&D in comparison with 1,5 to 2% for the biggest multinational companies. This could lead to competitive disadvantages in the long run.

Overall, however, there is no reason to be pessimistic, because the Danish dairy and slaughtering industries are very strong. They are also part of a very strong agro-industrial complex, and this ought to be able to support their competitiveness in the long run. The Danish agro-industrial complex is made up of a number of widely different industries which interact and support each other. A competitive advantage of the slaughtering industry is, for example, often said to be its high-quality products. This is certainly due to high-quality processing of the meat, but also to high-quality raw materials from the farming industry as well as high-quality cooling systems and machinery. The farming industry in turn needs high-quality machines, fertilizers and pesticides. The industries in the agro-industrial complex tend to put pressure on each other to continuously improve their respective products and processes. This in turn enables the individual industries to enhance their international competitiveness. In this way

Table 12

The Danish food industry, 1988

	Employment[1]	%	GDP at factor cost[2]	%
Slaughtering and meat products	27,6	30,4	7,5	30,5
Dairy products	9,0	9,9	4,2	17,1
Fishing	10,4	11,5	2,3	9,3
Vegetable oil products	2,4	2,6	0,7	2,8
Cereal and baking products	18,8	20,7	3,0	12,2
Sugar and chocolate products	6,2	6,8	2,3	9,3
Brewing	7,2	7,9	2,2	8,9
Other	9,2	10,1	2,4	9,8
Total	90,7	100,0	24,6	100,0

[1] In thousands.
[2] In billion DKR.
Source: Danmarks Statistik, national accounts.

the agro-industrial complex is setting the stage for the generation of a stream of innovations and continuous growth.

The employment and growth prospects for the dairy and slaughtering industries as such are difficult to evaluate. The growth prospects may not be bad, if the agro-industrial complex can maintain and even strengthen its competitiveness. However, the prospects for employment in the two industries are probably for stagnation. Concentration has strengthened the competitive position of the two industries, but it has at the same time also led to rationalization. This has made the industries much more efficient but has also reduced employment. There is no reason why the rationalization process should stop given current technological developments in factory and office automation equipment.

The employment prospects in traditional core food-product areas like the dairy and slaughtering industries may to a certain extent be offset by the trend towards more prepared foods. New segments in canned and frozen foods may therefore increase, which could to a certain extent compensate for lost jobs in other sectors if strong market positions could be developed in these segments. On the other hand, the bulk of the market for the next years is still expected to be fresh non-prepared food products.

The textiles and clothing industry

The Danish textiles and clothing industry employed 38 000 people in 1988. It is not one of the biggest, but is still an important industry in the Danish economy. About 50% of the production is exported, the biggest markets being the other Scandinavian countries. In this sense, the Danish textiles and clothing industry has managed to find an international 'niche'.

The Danish textiles and clothing industry produces a wide variety of products such as carpets, cloth, ropes, fishing nets, leather products, shoes, knitwear and clothing. The most important of these industries in terms of employment are knitwear and clothing, which account for about 60% of employment. Some of the industries like spinning, synthetic fibres, carpet and shoe manufacturing consist of a few, but larger, firms. The knitwear and clothing industries on the other hand are fragmented industries, i.e. consisting of many smaller firms. The average firm size in the knitwear and clothing industries was 30 employees in 1988.

The textiles and clothing industry would normally be considered to have few chances of survival in a high-cost country like Denmark. The development in employment in the industry has also followed a pattern similar to other European

countries. Employment is today only 50% of the 1965 level. Difficulties exist, particularly in areas characterized by relatively labour-intensive homogeneous mass production, like spinning. Industries like knitwear and clothing have not been affected to the same extent, but employment has not increased either.

The Danish knitwear and clothing industry is concentrated in the county of Ringkøbing in western Jutland. The indications are that a textiles industrial complex, in some ways similar to but on a smaller scale than the one in the Emilio Romagna and Prato regions in Italy, exists in this part of the country. Here, an environment adapted to this kind of industry, including companies which mutually reinforce each other, has developed. This means that the employment in the textile and clothing industry in the county of Ringkøbing in western Jutland has increased slightly over the period 1965-89, whereas it has decreased in the rest of the country. Employment in the textile and clothing industry in Ringkøbing now accounts for more than 40% of employment in the Danish textile and clothing industry.

The Danish textiles and clothing industry has in recent years lost market share on the traditional Scandinavian markets. Sales have not declined, but have not grown as fast as sales of other exporters, for example Italian companies, to Scandinavia. On the other hand, Danish exports to the rest of the Community have increased in recent years. It should also be noted that Danish textiles and clothing companies have never received any subsidies, as has been the case in some other EC countries. It is a highly efficient industry which has always been exposed to competition. The Danish textiles and clothing industry may be in a good position compared with subsidized textiles and clothing industries in other EC countries, should those subsidies be abolished.

It cannot be concluded that the Danish textiles and clothing industry will decline into insignificance, even though it is a fragmented, mature industry exposed to competition from other European as well as low-cost NICs and East European countries. Time has shown that a Danish textiles industry can exist and be competitive. The market potential in the Community is in principle very big and the growth prospects of the industry could be quite good. However, it is very hard to say which way the development will go. Much will depend on subsidizing policies and the future of the international Multifibre Arrangement.

Pharmaceuticals

Globally seen, the pharmaceuticals industry has very good growth prospects. It is a research-intensive and turbulent industry. The EC pharmaceuticals industry spent 15% of its turnover on R&D in 1988. The leading companies are multinational European or American companies, but due to high R&D expenses even these companies have specialized their research in certain areas.

The Danish pharmaceuticals industry employed about 12 500 people in 1990 (MEFA). Employment has increased 4,7% per year since 1980. The pharmaceuticals industry exports about 85% of its production and is one of the biggest Danish export industries. Indeed, Denmark is one of the biggest exporters of pharmaceuticals. Only Switzerland has higher exports of pharmaceuticals per capita. The most important companies are Novo-Nordisk, Alfred Benzon, Lundbeck, and Løvens Kemiske Fabrik, and the most important product groups are insulin, antibiotics, vitamins, diuretics, sulphonamides and psychopharmaceuticals.

The Danish health system has played a key role in the development of a pharmaceuticals industry. The Danish health system is among the most efficient in the world, and sets very high standards. This has often enabled the companies to gain an advantage in their product development. The traditionally very fierce competition between the Danish pharmaceuticals companies has been important in creating a pressure to innovate. The Danish pharmaceuticals companies are, however, by international standards relatively small, and there are some indications that they spend relatively less on R&D than is common in the industry. The question arises whether the Danish pharmaceuticals companies have the critical mass necessary to be competitive in the long run.

Danish top managers in the pharmaceuticals industry recognize these problems, and point to the need for further internationalization and cooperation. Only in this way will it be possible for the pharmaceuticals industry to avoid being reduced to a regional industry. However, if such measures are successful, and if the supporting structures are improved, particularly as far as public R&D is concerned, and higher education, then there is a considerable potential for higher employment and exports. The Danish Association of Pharmaceuticals Manufacturers estimates that employment could increase from 23 000 in 1990 to 45 000 directly and indirectly employed persons in 2000 (Kaare Madsen and MEFA, 1992).

Sea transport

The Danish sea-transport industry is one of the biggest in the world and in the Community Denmark has a bigger sea-transport industry than countries like France, Spain and the Netherlands. The industry employed about 19 000 people in 1990 (including support functions). It is one of the biggest export industries in Denmark, accounting for about 10% of Danish exports of goods and services in 1990.

In the 1980s the international sea-transport industry was under much pressure. The demand for sea-transport services fell among other things due to low economic growth at the beginning of the decade. The building of ships continued despite the low demand for sea-transport services. This created overcapacity and a very competitive market for sea-transport services. The traditional sea-transport nations in Western Europe as a consequence saw a big reduction of their fleets. Some companies went bankrupt, while others registered their ships in Panama, Liberia and similar countries with more liberal standards for taxation and crew.

Denmark saw its fleet reduced by about 20% over the decade. This is a relatively small reduction compared to other EC countries. The establishment of the Danish International Ship register (DIS) in 1988 played a major role in this respect. Ships registered in DIS profit from more liberal rules for taxation and the crew. It has recently been argued that DIS is in conflict with EC competition rules in intra-EC transportation.

The Danish sea-transport industry consists of about 300 companies. However, the concentration is quite high. The 10 biggest companies operate about 90% of the tonnage. The two biggest companies are A. P. Møller and Lauritzen. The industry is extremely international: 90% of the Danish sea-transport services are international between third countries. The Danish sea-transport industry is very competitive and is interested in a total liberalization of the market for sea-transport services. However, particularly Third World countries have been proponents for increased protection for their 'infant industries'. The future of the Danish sea-transport industry is closely connected to the international developments in this area.

The Danish sea-transport industry has close interrelations with the Danish shipbuilding industry. Two of the biggest Danish shipyards are even owned by sea-transport companies. The transport companies often cooperate closely with the Danish shipyards in the development of new innovative ships enabling them to become even more competitive. The relationship between the Danish sea-transport and shipbuilding industries will be discussed further in the next section.

Shipbuilding

Internationally seen, Denmark is one of the largest ship-building nations in the world. In 1990 Danish shipyards delivered 2,5% of the ships built world-wide. Only Japan (43%), South Korea (21,8%), Taiwan (4,2%) and the former Yugoslavia (2,9%) were larger producers. In deliveries to the Community the unified Germany was a larger producer, but the Danish shipbuilding industry was larger than the Italian, French and Spanish.

The demand for new ships started to decrease in the mid-1970s. This has led to a heavy reduction in shipbuilding capacity in a number of European countries. On average, the EC countries thus reduced their shipbuilding capacity by 60% in the period 1978 to 1988. In Denmark, the capacity was reduced by 42%. Japan saw a reduction in its capacity by 48%, whereas South Korea was able to increase its capacity by 15% in the period.

The Danish shipbuilding industry basically consists of six major shipyards. The dominant activity is the building of new ships, whereas repairs are of minor importance. The Danish shipyards build a wide variety of ships like oil tankers, container ships, bulk carriers, fishing ships, ferry boats, chemical tankers, etc. As mentioned, the Danish sea-transport companies often place orders for new innovative ships with Danish shipyards in order to achieve an advantage over their competitors. This of course also benefits the shipyards. Furthermore, the Danish shipyards have developed specialized skills in several types of ships, and often build larger series of 'high-tech' ships, which need only a relatively small crew to operate. Danish shipyards have had quite high R&D activities.

In 1990 the Danish shipyards employed 9 200 people, had sales of DKR 6,7 billion, and orders worth DKR 20 billion. In the Community, only the shipyards in unified Germany had orders of a higher accumulated value. The employment level at the Danish shipyards was, on the other hand, only one third of the level in the mid-1970s, illustrating the big reduction which has taken place in the industry. In this connection, however, it must also be considered that the shipyards today, to a larger extent than earlier, are using subcontractors.

The Danish shipbuilding industry is today one of the most modern and efficient in the world. The industry has, as in almost all countries, been subsidized by the government due to the very difficult period it has been through. However, the Danish subsidies have on average been smaller than in other countries, and the subsidies were not given to the shipyards, but in the financing provided for the sea-transport companies. In this way, competition between the shipyards was maintained and the risk of subsidizing inefficient production was reduced. The Danish shipyards have therefore been under constant pressure to innovate and become more efficient. This has been a major factor behind the current very strong international position.

The prospects for the Danish shipbuilding industry are not easy to evaluate. The developments in two particular areas seem of critical importance. Firstly, much will depend on subsidizing policies globally. The German shipyards in the former GDR are likely to be a significant threat in this respect. Of the ships built in Danish shipyards, 70 to 80% are purchased by companies in the Danish sea-transport industry. However, the competition between Danish shipyards, and between Danish and foreign shipyards, is very strong. It is not certain that a Danish sea-transport company will always place an order with a Danish shipyard. This is the case even for the yards owned by sea-transport companies. Therefore, there is no doubt that the new shipyards in the former GDR will become strong competitors. The stronger competition is already being felt and the outlook is not nearly as bright as just a year ago. Secondly, the future of the Danish sea-transport industry will be important. The tendencies towards increased protectionism in international sea transport could also be a threat to the Danish shipbuilding industry.

The business services industry

In the national accounts, the business services industry encompasses a very heterogeneous group of industries like cleaning, security, training, consulting, data-processing services, advertising etc. Some of these industries are relatively mature, while others rank among the high-growth industries. Many of the business services industries would merit a separate analysis, but the statistics describing the area are not very well developed. However, it is a very important area, which cannot be ignored.

In Denmark, the business services field was one of the fastest growing areas in the 1980s. Employment increased by 3,7% per year in the period 1980-90. Business services accounted for 5,5% of total employment in Denmark in 1990, i.e. as much as agriculture and more than the food-products industry.

The business services industry is expected to be a big provider of jobs in the future. It can be calculated that business services increased their share of input to manufacturing industry from 1,3% in 1966 to 4,4% in 1987. There are several important and related trends behind this development. Firstly, there is a tendency for companies to externalize non-core functions. Companies have found that such 'lean production techniques' help to reduce costs and increase flexibility in an environment which is becoming more and more turbulent. Secondly, the increasing sophistication of business will make it necessary for companies to make increasing use of specialized skills, which would particularly seem to increase the need for consulting and training services. Thirdly, the diffusion of information technology will create many new information services products.

Business services is expected to be one of the high-growth industries of the future. As with many other services industries, it is expected to become more international. Many Danish consulting firms have already been acquired by foreign companies or have established international strategic alliances. The internationalization will undoubtedly also improve the quality of services. Overall, the business services industry is likely to become one of the big providers of new jobs in the future.

References

Cecchini report, 'Cost of non-Europe', *European Economy*, 1988.

Dalum, Bent, Møller, Kim, Jørgensen, Ulrik, Valentin, Finn, *Internationalisering og Erhvervsudvikling*, Notat, Industri- og Handelsstyrelsen, Copenhagen, 1991.

Det Blå Danmark, Danish Ministry of Industry, March, 1991.

Evaluering af lov nr. 365 af 10. juni 1987 om tilskud til produktudvikling i jordbruget, Jordbrugsdirektoratet, Danish Ministry of Agriculture, 1991.

Finansredegørelse 92, Ministry of Finance, 1992.

Fusioner og Virksomhedsovertagelser 1985-91, Danish Council for Competition Control, Copenhagen.

Madsen, Kåre, MEFA, *Dansk medicinindustri år 2002*, MEFA, 1992.

Madsen, Poul Thøis, 'Mysteriet om den forsvundne produktivitet', *Samfundsøkonomen*, No 5, 1991.

Madsen, Ole Øhlenschlæger, *Virksomhedsovertagelser og fusioner i dansk industri*, Nyt Nordisk Forlag, Arnold Busck, Copenhagen, 1983.

Maskell, Peter, *Nyetableringer i industrien*, Handelshøjskolens Forlag, Copenhagen, 1992.

Nielsen, Kent T., 'Industrielle Netværk', Ph.D. dissertation, Århus University, Institute of Management, 1991.

Panorama of EC industry 1991-92, Commission of the European Communities, 1991.

Porter, Michael E., *Competitive strategy*, The Free Press, 1980.

Porter, Michael E., *Competitive advantage*, The Free Press, 1985.

Porter, Michael E., *The competitive advantage of nations*, Macmillan, 1990.

Schultz, Poul, Strandskov, Jesper, Vestergård Harald, *Hvor internationale er danske virksomheder*, Managements Erhvervspolitiske Forum, 1986.

Trends i afsætningen af jordbrugsprodukter det kommende årti, Jordbrugsdirektoratet, Danish Ministry of Agriculture, July 1989.

Walsh, Vivien, 'Technology, competitiveness, and the special problems of small countries', *Science, technology, and industry review*, OECD, Paris, 1987.

The machine that changed the world, MIT study on the future of the automobile, 1990.

Chapter 4

The Danish financial system

4.1. Structure

The Danish financial sector can be broadly looked at in terms of the banking system, mortgage credit institutions, insurance companies and pension funds, and the Stock Exchange.

4.1.1. Banking system

The banking sector was historically divided into savings banks (the first of which was founded in 1810 as a depository institution for small savings) and commercial banks (the first founded in 1846 to finance local trade). There was a rapid increase in the number of banks established up to 1920, but since then the trend has been towards a greater concentration in larger units with broad branch networks. Over the years the distinction between the activities of the commercial banks and savings banks has become blurred, with commercial banks offering services to the public at large, not only trade and industry, and attracting deposits from the public to the extent that by the 1950s their deposits were larger than those with savings banks. At the same time, savings banks have switched their assets progressively from holdings of fixed-interest securities to overdrafts and loans to individuals. From 1975, savings banks were allowed to conduct all types of banking business. The development of savings banks culminated with a change in the law from 1 January 1989 which enabled those banks which had previously been non-profit-making self-governing institutions to become public limited companies.

Until recently, the basic structure of the banking system has been of six to eight, largely nation-wide banks, a similar number of medium-sized banks and a substantial number of small local commercial banks, savings banks and cooperatives. There was a progressive trend towards capital concentration in the commercial bank sector in the 1980s with mergers between Jyske Bank and Finansbanken in 1981, Sjaellandske Bank and Frederiksborg Bank in 1983 and Provinsbank and Kronebanken in 1985. In the second half of 1989, two mega-mergers took place whereby six of the eight largest banks formed two large banks — Den Danske Bank (made up of Den Danske Bank, Handelsbanken and Provinsbanken) and Unibank (comprising SDS, Privat-

banken and Andelsbanken). Thus at end-1991 these two large banks accounted for nearly 60% of total assets with Den Danske Bank at 35% and Unibank 25% (see Graph 25). Although these two new banks are dominant on the Danish market, they only rank 40th and 50th respectively in European banking terms. A significant reason for the mergers, along with the desire to be better equipped to compete in the emerging European financial market, was the perceived high level of operating costs. Since the main Danish banks have extensive branch networks (see Table 13), with the number of inhabitants per bank branch lower only in Belgium, Luxembourg and Spain, a reduction in the number of branches is one method of reducing costs.

Although savings banks had previously been regarded as a separate category, since the middle of the 1970s they have been permitted to engage in all types of banking business including foreign business. Thus, they are now as a group practically indistinguishable from the commercial banks. The great majority of the 115 savings banks (with 695 branches) in Denmark are small local operations. Their number has been falling significantly with local savings banks, affected by weakness in agricultural earnings, being in most cases taken over by larger savings banks. In general, the smaller banks have been losing market share. There are several large savings banks, one of which, Bikuben, rivals other banks in size. The five largest savings banks accounted in 1991 for nearly 90% of total assets of this subsector.

However, traditional close ties with personal customers remain, with the result that almost half of total lending and more than half total deposits relate to the personal sector. About 15% of total lending of savings banks consists of long-term secured mortgage loans. Overdraft lending has increased rapidly in recent years as savings banks have moved into the traditional areas of commercial banks.

Table 13

Number of commercial and savings banks in Denmark

	1980	1985	1990	1992[1]
Total	249	230	201	197
Number of branches	3 656	3 493	3 002	

[1] Preliminary estimate.

NB: In 1992 there were two foreign banks, six foreign branches and eight banks in Greenland and the Faeroe Islands. Of the remaining 181 commercial and savings banks, 70 were small savings banks with working capital of less than DKR 100 million.

Source: Danish financial supervisory authority's annual reports.

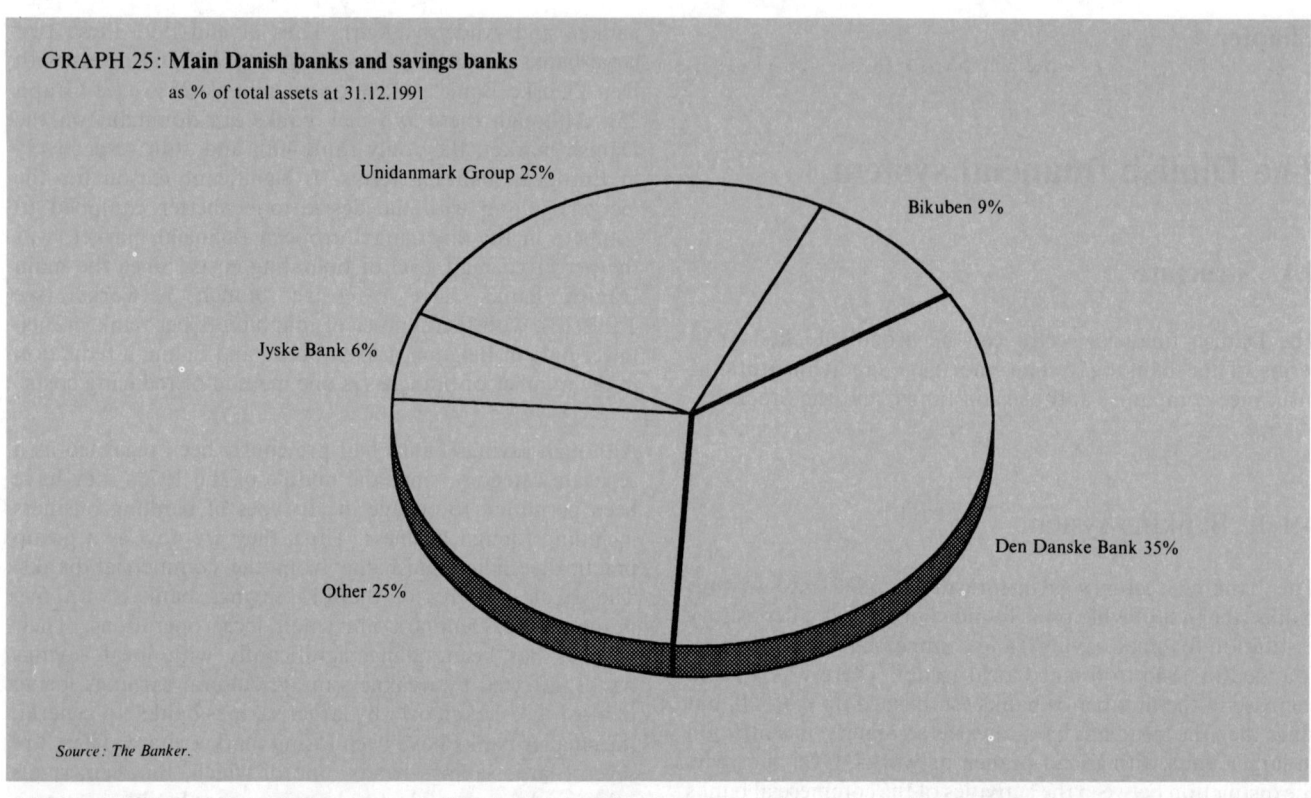

GRAPH 25: **Main Danish banks and savings banks**
as % of total assets at 31.12.1991

Unidanmark Group 25%

Bikuben 9%

Jyske Bank 6%

Den Danske Bank 35%

Other 25%

Source: The Banker.

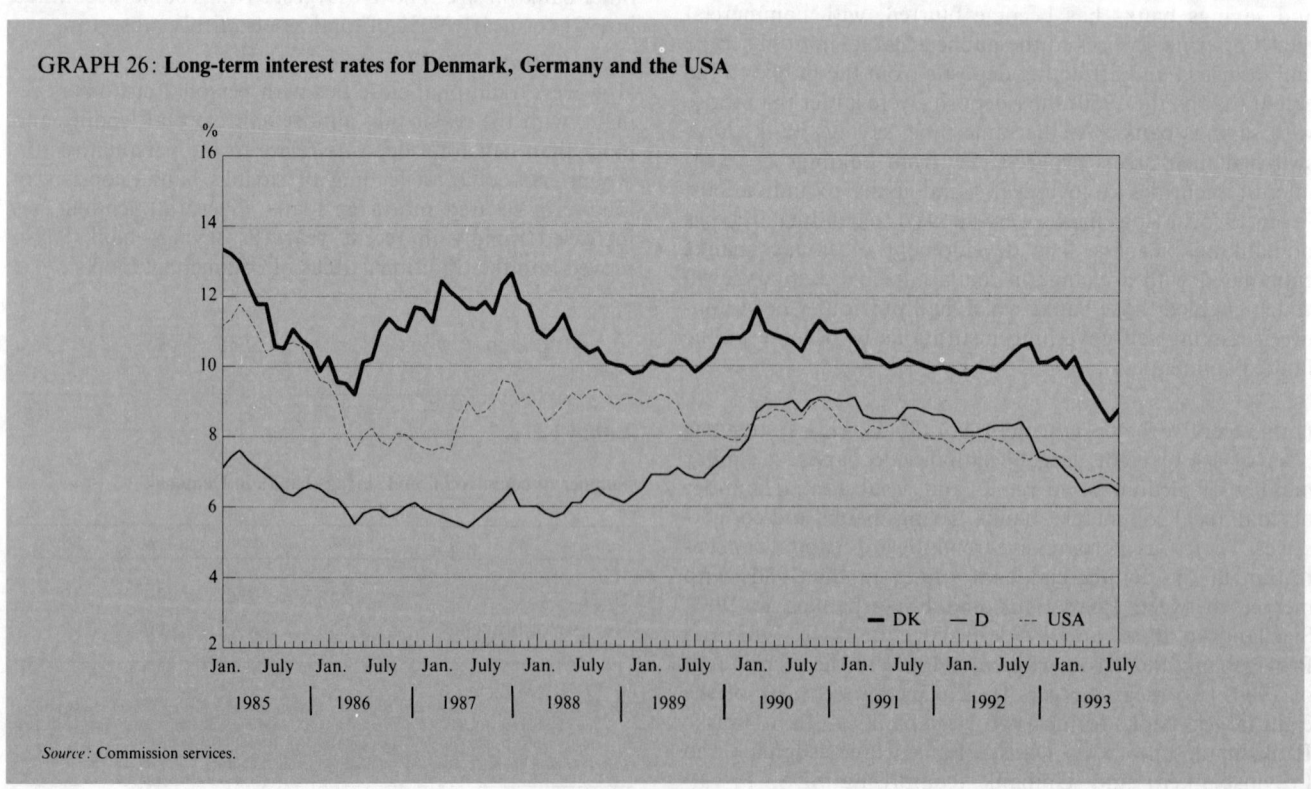

GRAPH 26: **Long-term interest rates for Denmark, Germany and the USA**

%

16

14

12

10

8

6

4

2

Jan. July Jan. July Jan. July Jan. July Jan. July Jan. July Jan. July Jan. July Jan. July

1985 | 1986 | 1987 | 1988 | 1989 | 1990 | 1991 | 1992 | 1993

— DK — D --- USA

Source: Commission services.

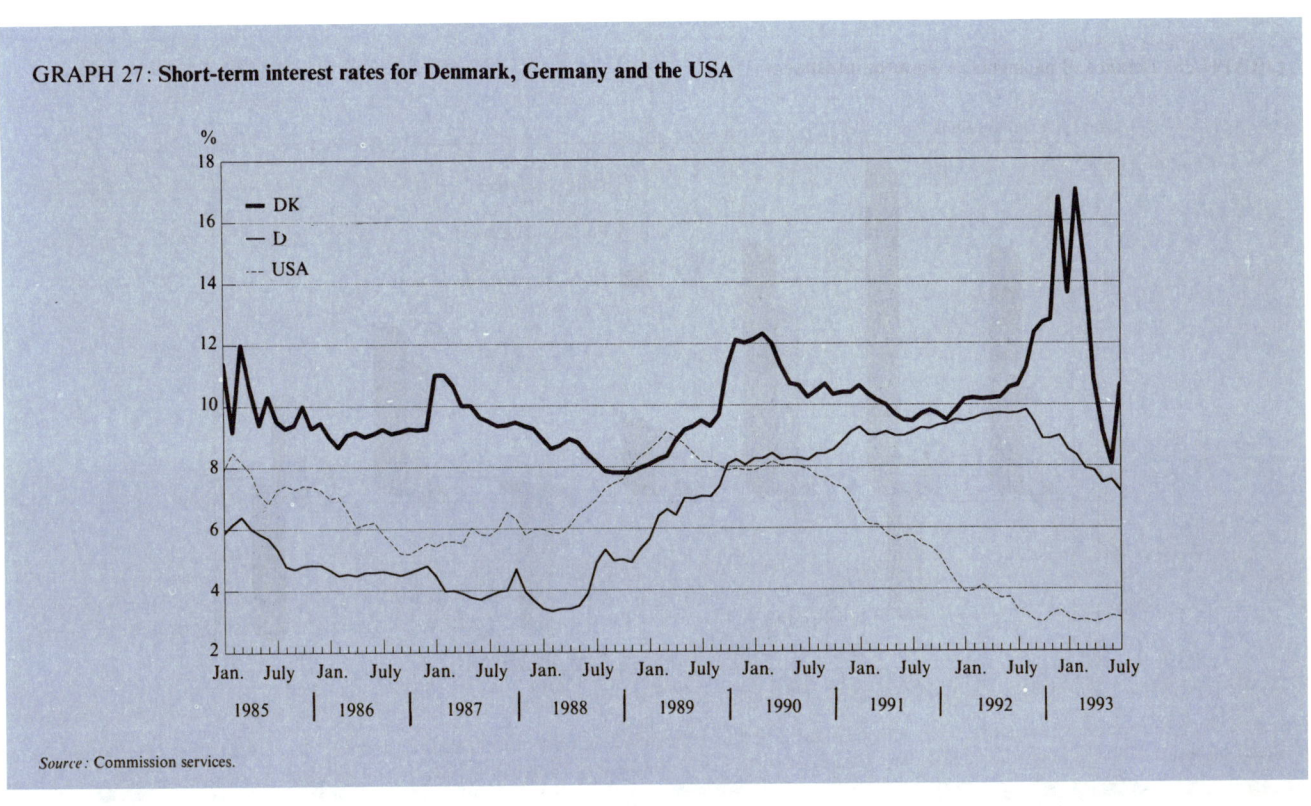

GRAPH 27: **Short-term interest rates for Denmark, Germany and the USA**

%

— DK
— D
--- USA

Jan. July Jan. July Jan. July Jan. July Jan. July Jan. July Jan. July Jan. July Jan. July

1985 | 1986 | 1987 | 1988 | 1989 | 1990 | 1991 | 1992 | 1993

Source: Commission services.

While international cost comparisons are difficult, given different financial structures and forms of banking activity, surveys on financial institutions' costs by OECD show that total operating costs as a proportion of total assets were relatively high in Danish financial institutions. One of the causes is the fact that retail banking in Denmark makes up a relatively large proportion of the financial institutions' overall activities. Danish institutions conduct a higher proportion of business with private customers than is the case elsewhere and the structure of business there is marked by a large number of small firms. However, rationalization in bank networks of the new big banks is expected to bring down costs significantly. Additionally, Nationalbank feels that the high cost levels of banks reflect the fact that, for many years, interest rates have played only a minor role in the competition for private customers with the steep increase in marginal tax rates since the beginning of the 1970s, together with full inclusion of interest income and full deduction of interest expenses in taxable income, contributing to this trend. The result has been that banks have been

encouraged to compete on services instead of on interest rates. From 1986, tax reforms have probably increased price awareness and increased pressure on banks to cut costs.

Lending is broadly spread over all sectors of trade and industry. Non-business advances account for over one third of total domestic lending. Over a half of deposits with banks are accounted for by the private non-business sector.

Of particular interest in the Danish case has been the active encouragement, since the end of the 1970s, of firms raising money abroad by the maintenance of significant interest-rate differentials (see Graphs 26 and 27). The result has been that the accumulated external obligations of the business sector since 1983 in terms of portfolio disinvestment and other borrowing has been more than four times that of the increase in external indebtedness of public authorities. Thus, while there is a general outflow of direct investment, this has generally been swamped by large inflows of portfolio and other long-term investment (see Graph 28).

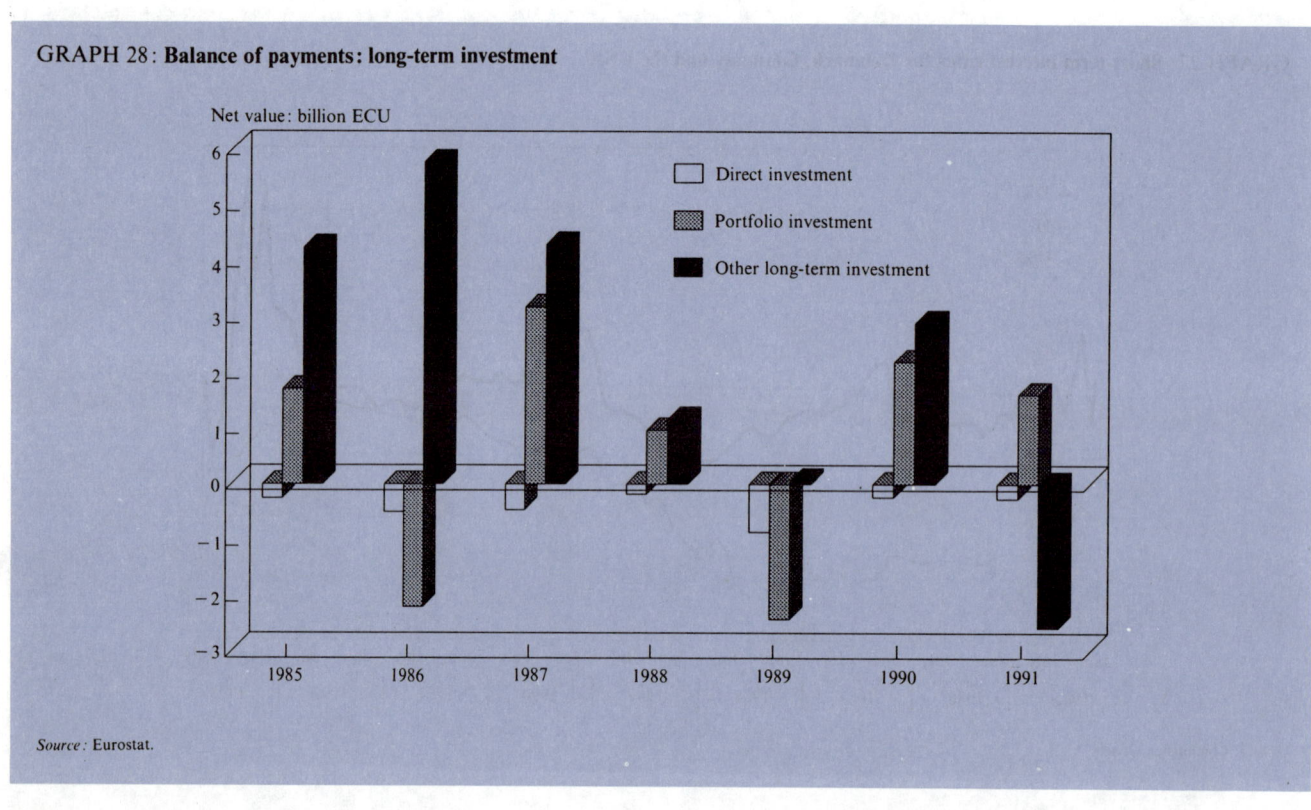

GRAPH 28: **Balance of payments: long-term investment**

Net value: billion ECU

Direct investment

Portfolio investment

Other long-term investment

Source: Eurostat.

4.1.2. Mortgage credit institutions

A particular feature of the Danish market is the specialized role of mortgage credit institutions. For over a century Denmark has had an active mortgage bond market. The system was first established in 1797 and the principles were basically established in the mid-19th century. Individual borrowers from an association and the members are liable for the mortgages raised. When a borrower requires finance, his property is valued and a loan can then be granted. Against the security of the mortgage deeds, the association issues bonds which are sold on the stock exchange at market price with the proceeds going to the borrower. They are issued at fixed or variable interest rates and are normally callable at face value. Mortgage bonds have traded at a small spread against government bonds. It was this market, rather than the national debt market, which provided the Danish bond market with its bench mark issue until recently: the 9% 2006 bond. Only recently has this role been taken

over by government 9% bullet bonds. Mortgage credit bonds generally account for over 60% of total turnover. Mortgage loans, which remain on the property purchased, and are taken on by any new owner, are matched exactly with bonds issued in the public market by mortgage credit agencies: straightforward pass-through securities. The bonds traded on the stock exchange which were issued to finance each loan can be identified exactly. These bonds carry the same interest rate as the mortgage loan. The length of loans and limits on the total loan amount that can be financed by bonds are set down in legislation. Generally, limits tend to be 80% and loans are normally granted for 20 years although since 1990, 30-year loans are possible. Interest and repayment of capital are repaid each three months. The mortgage credit institutions make money on their arrangement fees and on investment returns on their reserve funds. The three Danish mortgage credit institutions, which are products of a long history of mergers, run an oligopolistic market which covers 95% of all building. Kreditforeningen Danmark and Nykredit each have a market share of around 40% while Byggeriets Realkreditfond has around 20%.

The first banking directive of 1987 allowed foreign mortgage credit institutions to operate in Denmark and previous rules whereby the authorities could refuse establishment in Denmark of foreign companies for economic reasons lapsed. With the adoption of the second banking directive, the monopoly of mortgage credit associations to grant loans on property mortgages was abolished and other institutions are now permitted to engage in this business. These legislative developments spurred on horizontal mergers with Nykredit merging with the insurance company Tryg in 1991, an arrangement that was recently unwound. A further merger was planned with Unibanken in 1992 to create a 'financial supermarket' and Denmark's largest financial institution, but because of losses at Unibank in 1990 the merger was called off.

The differential (Graph 29) between government bonds and mortgage credit bonds has risen significantly and the margin between the benchmark government bond and the corresponding mortgage credit bond is now over 1 percentage point. This may reflect doubts on the creditworthiness of mortgage bonds in a depressed economy. However, it has been suggested that other factors may be more important in explaining this spread, in particular the conversion option for borrowers, the fact that mortgage bonds come in small series and the annuity loan characteristic of the bonds, which make them less familiar to foreign investors. It is felt that legislative relaxation in conditions can be availed of by mortgage credit institutions to modernize the range of bonds available and develop products which take lenders' requirements into account.

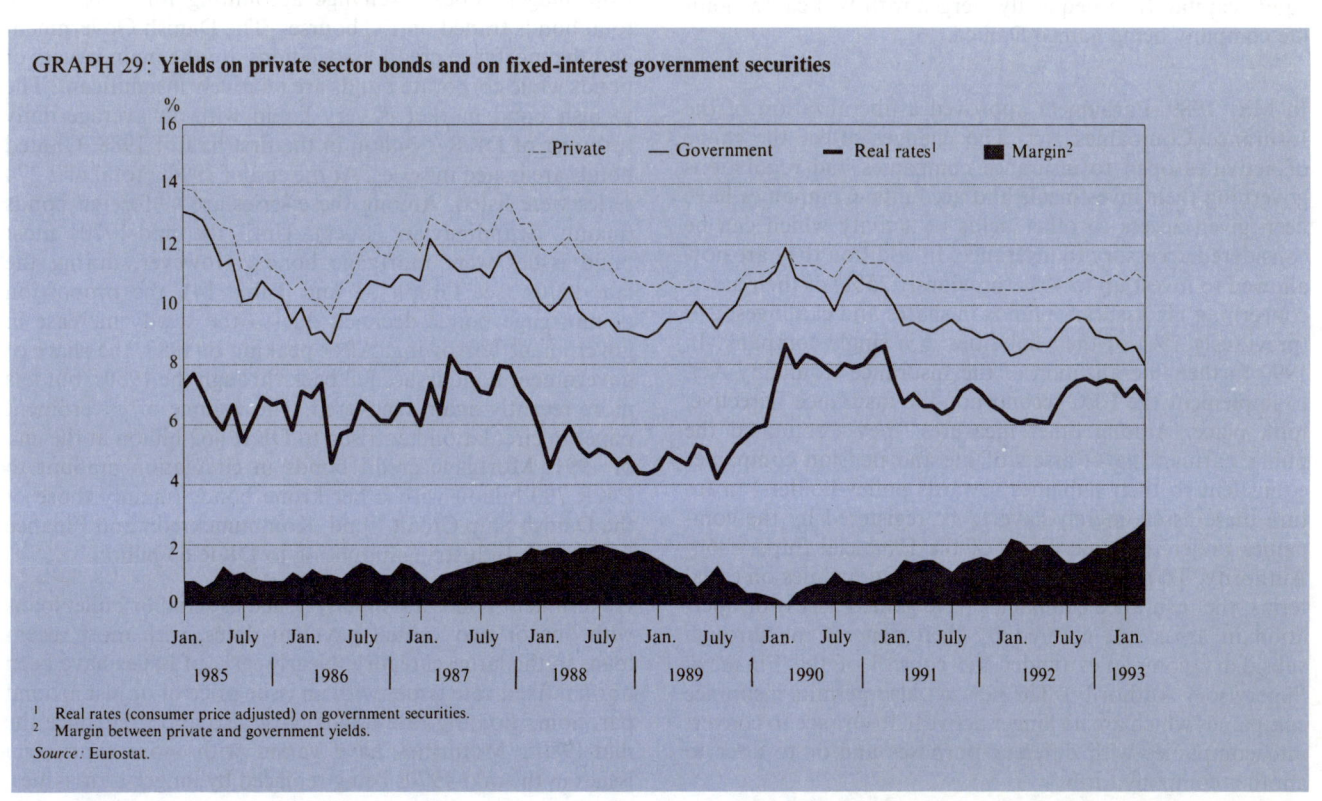

GRAPH 29: **Yields on private sector bonds and on fixed-interest government securities**

--- Private — Government — Real rates[1] ■ Margin[2]

[1] Real rates (consumer price adjusted) on government securities.
[2] Margin between private and government yields.
Source: Eurostat.

4.1.3. Insurance companies and pension funds

To safeguard the separation of funds in long-term life and pension policies from shorter-term non-life insurance activities, Danish legislation requires that the two forms of insurance be conducted by separate companies. In 1991, according to statistics from the Financial Supervisory Authority there were 195 non-life companies (64 limited companies, 40 foreign companies and 91 mutual companies). The top five non-life companies (see Graph 30) accounted for nearly 60% of gross premium income (Hafnia 15%, Baltica 14%, Alm. Brand 12%, Topdanmark 10% and Tryg 8%). The non-life firms mostly form part of large insurance groups together with life companies. There were 26 life assurance companies (20 limited companies, two foreign and three mutual companies plus the State life company) in 1991, the top five life companies representing 75% of gross premiums of DKR 17 billion (Danica 25%, PFA 23%, Kom. Pens. 10%, Tryg 8% and Hafnia 8%). In May 1990, the privatization of the Danish State life assurance institute (Statsanstalten for Livsforsikring) was approved in Parliament. Under the terms of this legislation the institute, which was founded in 1842 and in 1989 had a combined premium income of DKR 2,9 billion, about 400 000 policy-holders and a market share of about 25%, was converted into a public company, with a holding company owning all the equity capital. It subsequently merged with Baltica, the joint life company being named Danica.

In May 1989, Parliament approved a liberalization of the Insurance Companies Act. The changes affect the range of activities open to insurance companies and regulations governing their investments and accounts. Companies have been given access to other fields of activity which can be considered accessory to insurance. In addition they are now allowed to invest up to 40% (previously 25%) of their assets concerning life assurance funds in shares and can invest 2% (previously 1%) of their liabilities in a single company. In 1990 further liberalization of the Insurance Company Act, to implement the EEC second non-life insurance Directive, took place. Among other measures, they terminated the public earmarking of assets of life and pension companies equivalent to their liabilities towards policy-holders; in future these assets merely have to be registered by the companies under the supervision of the Financial Supervisory Authority. To put banks and insurance companies on equal terms, the insurance companies have gained access of operation in areas not covered by their concessions through subsidiary companies (under the control of the Financial Supervisory Authority). The new act also permits insurance companies which are no longer active in insurance to convert into companies with different purposes and/or to alter to another company form.

Most assets of life insurance companies are held in the form of bonds, with mortgage deed bonds representing 52% of balance sheet total, index-linked bonds 13% and government bonds 2%. Listed Danish shares represent a further 7% of assets.

Non-life companies hold a smaller proportion of their assets in terms of bonds, with mortgage credit deeds representing 23% and government bonds 7%. Deposits and liquid funds represent 5% of balance sheet total while total Danish shares and capital holdings account for 31% (of which 22% represents participating interests in subsidiaries or associates).

In 1991 there were 1 462 000 private pension schemes in Denmark, almost equally divided into lump sum pension schemes and schemes with annuities. Premium income of all schemes was DKR 13 billion. Lump sum pension schemes were principally with banks, while two thirds of annuity schemes were with insurance companies.

4.1.4. The Stock Exchange

The Danish domestic capital market is dominated by bonds. Copenhagen is the world's ninth largest bond market measured by the volume of bonds in circulation with the Copenhagen Stock Exchange accounting for 10% of the total bonds traded on EC bourses. The Danish Government and the mortgage credit associations are the main issuers of bonds while corporate bonds are relatively insignificant. The Danish bond market is very liquid with an average daily turnover of DKR 2 billion in the first half of 1988. Quoted bonds are issued in series. At the end of 1990 a total of 2 274 series were listed. Among these series are 49 foreign bonds (mainly Scandinavian issues). Until the mid-1970s most bond issues were mortgage bonds. However, during the late 1970s (see Graph 31 and Table 14), the proportion of mortgage bonds declined due to the steady increase in government borrowing. After peaking in 1983, the share of government bond issues fell back through the 1980s, but has more recently again recovered. The volume of government paper in circulation had risen to DKR 462 billion at the end of 1991. Mortgage credit bonds in circulation amount to DKR 790 billion with other krone bonds (mainly those of the Danish Ship Credit Fund, Kommunekredit and Finance for Danish Industry) amounting to DKR 63 billion.

Government bonds are mainly issued as serial or bullet loans with one or two annual payment dates, with most recent loans in the latter category. Nearly 90% of issues have been normal fixed-rate issues with an issue price of or just around par. Some floating rate bonds have also appeared since the mid-1980s. Maturities have varied with more short-term issues in the mid-1970s being replaced by longer-term issues.

GRAPH 30: **Main Danish insurance companies**

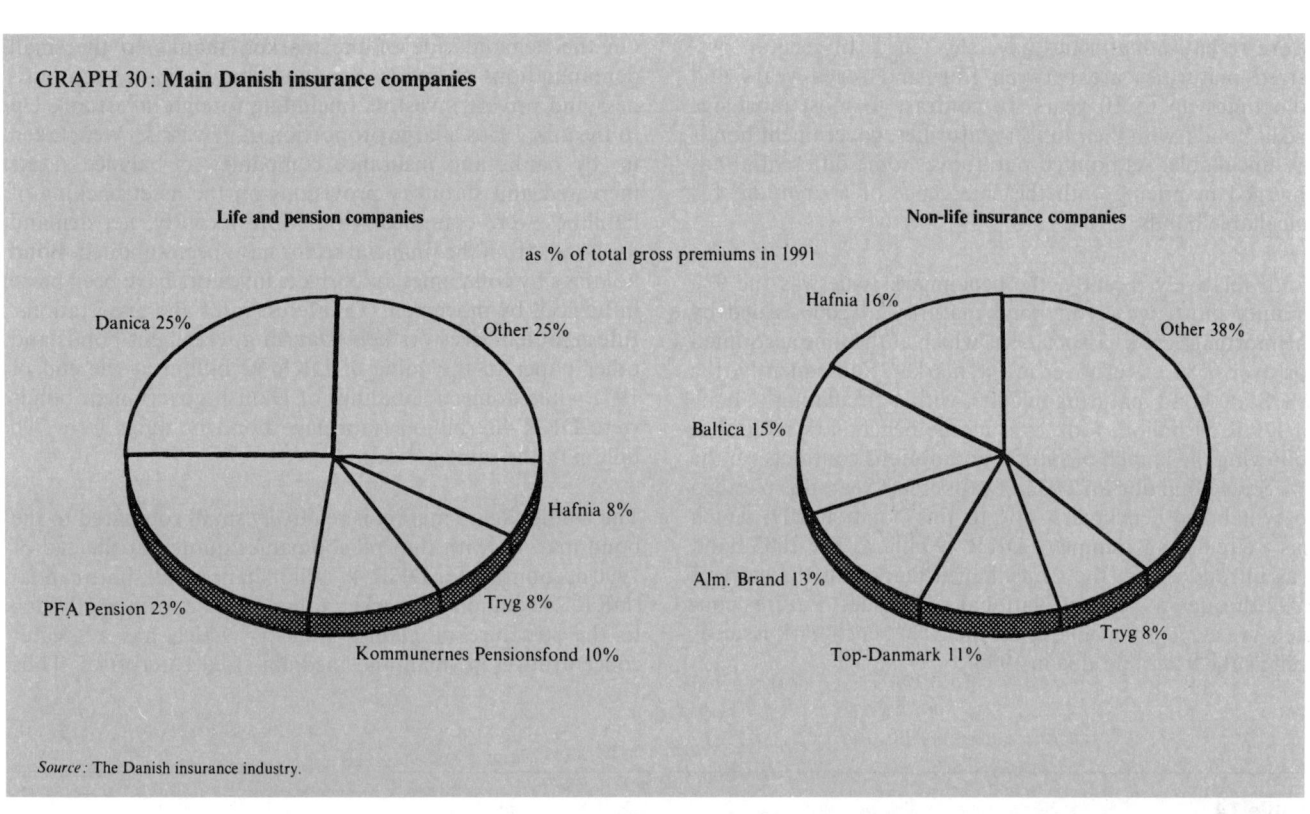

Life and pension companies

as % of total gross premiums in 1991

Non-life insurance companies

Danica 25%

Other 25%

Hafnia 8%

PFA Pension 23%

Tryg 8%

Kommunernes Pensionsfond 10%

Hafnia 16%

Other 38%

Baltica 15%

Alm. Brand 13%

Tryg 8%

Top-Danmark 11%

Source: The Danish insurance industry.

GRAPH 31: **Net issue of bonds (market value) by issuer**
Four-year moving average

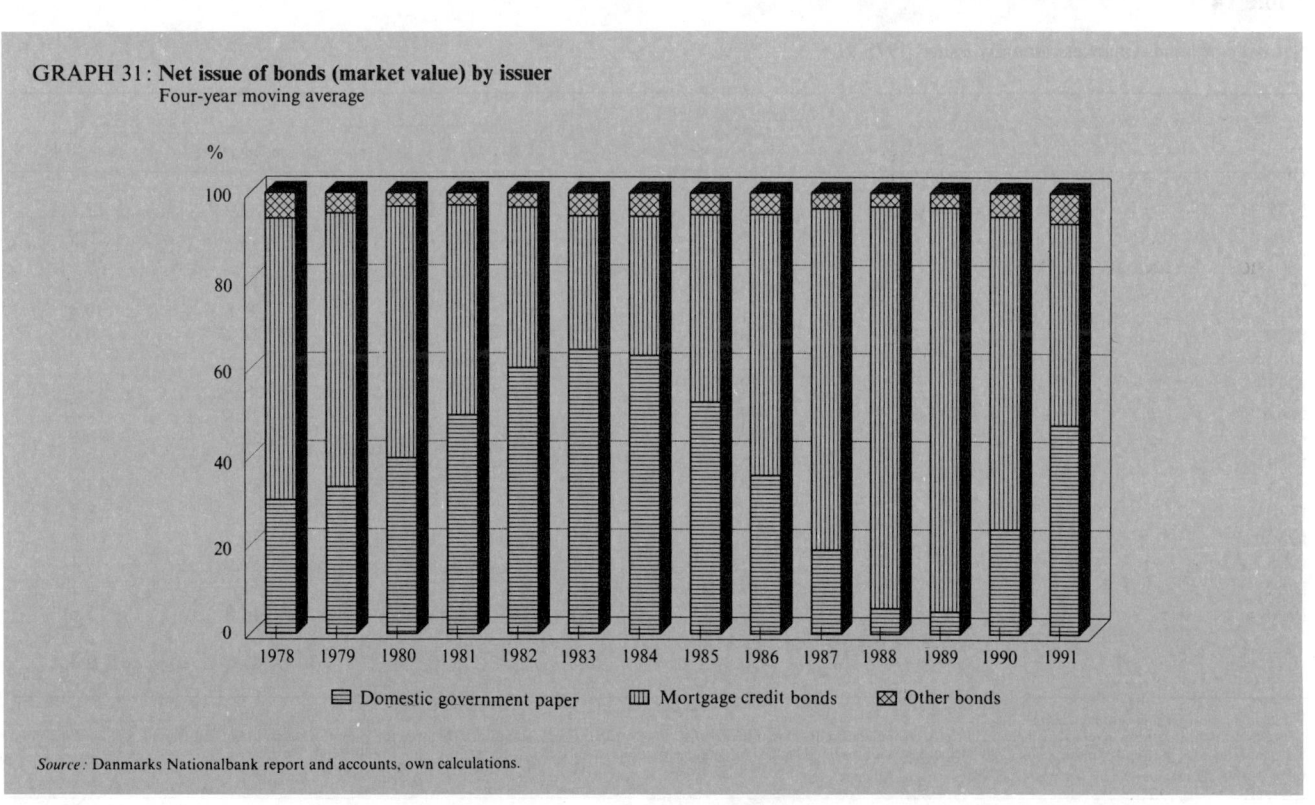

%

☰ Domestic government paper   ▥ Mortgage credit bonds   ⊠ Other bonds

Source: Danmarks Nationalbank report and accounts, own calculations.

More recently, maturities have shortened. In general, preferred maturities are between four and seven years and sometimes up to 10 years. In contrast to most mortgage credit bonds, with their longer maturities, government bonds are uncallable. As pointed out above, some differential has emerged in pricing with the emergence of a premium for uncallable bonds.

Until relatively recently, the benchmark issue was the 9% annuity mortgage credit bond maturity in 2006 issued by the mortgage credit associations which at the time accounted for over 65% of turnover in the market. Subsequently, the 9% State bond maturing in 2000, with a circulating volume of DKR 59 billion, took over as the benchmark issue, but following the launch of futures and options contracts on the 8% State bond due in 2003 in October last year, it is planned to switch the benchmark title to this bond shortly, which has a circulating volume of DKR 49 billion. The 2003 bond was introduced on the Copenhagen market at the start of 1992 through a series of Nationalbank issues. Futures contacts are currently available on the 2000 benchmark issue as well as the 9% bond due in 1995.

On the demand side of the market, thanks to the small denominations of bonds, the major buyers have been business and private investors (including foreign investors). Up to the mid-1980s a large proportion of new issues were taken up by banks and insurance companies as balance sheets increased and statutory provisions on the asset backing of liabilities were complied with. More recently, net demand for bonds from the financial sector have been subdued. Bond holdings by companies and private investors have been more influenced by movements in interest rates and expectations. International investors held Danish government bonds and other paper to the value of DKR 92 billion at the end of 1991 while domestic holdings of Danish government bonds were DKR 462 billion (mortgage bond holdings were 790 billion in the same period).

The Danish share market is relatively small compared to the bond market, with the 268 companies quoted at the end of 1990 accounting for DKR 43 billion in nominal share capital (DKR 245 billion at market value). This is principally due to the structure of Danish industry which has a greater concentration in small and medium-sized enterprises. Thus

Table 14

Net issue of bonds (market value) by issuer, 1975-91

	Domestic government paper[1]	Mortgage credit bonds	Bonds issued by other[2]	Total bond issue	
				Billion DKR	% of GDP
1975	5,7	20,1	1,5	27,3	12,6
1976	5,8	18,6	1,8	26,2	10,9
1977	9,6	17,0	1,9	28,5	10,2
1978	14,0	18,7	1,4	34,1	11,0
1979	11,1	21,1	0,4	32,6	9,4
1980	16,9	17,1	0,4	34,4	9,0
1981	29,0	11,5	1,7	42,2	12,7
1982	44,7	11,3	3,2	59,2	12,7
1983	53,0	27,5	6,3	86,8	16,9
1984	45,6	35,9	3,2	84,7	15,0
1985	24,0	60,4	2,8	87,2	14,1
1986	− 10,4	62,2	2,7	54,5	8,2
1987	− 7,3	53,0	1,0	46,7	6,8
1988	7,9	50,9	1,1	59,9	8,1
1989	19,2	10,2	1,7	31,1	4,1
1990	23,3	15,2	5,8	44,3	5,6
1991	50,3	20,9	5,9	77,1	9,3

[1] Including short-term government bonds.
[2] Bonds primarily issued by Kreditforeningen i Danmark (Kommunekredit), Finansieringsinstituttet for industri og Handværk (Finance for Danish Industry A/S), and Danmarks Skibskreditfond (Danish Ship Credit Fund). In the period 1980-88 about 80% of the bonds issued by other institutions were issued by the Danish Ship Credit Fund.
Source: Danmarks Nationalbank report and accounts, various volumes.

only a quarter of firms on the company register have nominal capital in excess of DKR 1 million. Of the companies quoted, the 20 largest had market capitalization of 66% of the total. The industrial sector represents over a third of market value of shares (with Carlsberg ranking first in terms of market value), while the banking and insurance sector is the next biggest sector followed by trade and services and shipping. The relaxation of listing requirement in 1982 and the introduction of a third market for small companies has stimulated issue activity.

On the basis of figures from the Danish Securities Centre, which operates the exchange's clearing and registration system, 65% of bond turnover was traded between two brokers compared with an average of 85% in the mid-1980s, with interbroker trading accounting for 40% of share turnover.

The Danish financial sector owns about 23% of shares in companies listed on the Stock Exchange. Private Danish investors own 37%, strategic cross holdings account for 20%, 10% are held by the two semi-official supplementary pension schemes (ATP and LD) while the remaining 10% is accounted for by non-residents.

The large relative size of the bond market and the long tradition of dealing with bonds not only by institutional investors, but also by private individuals, have resulted in a very large volume of transactions. In the 1970s it was suggested that the rather cumbersome handling of physical securities be replaced by a computer registration system whereby both interest payments, redemptions of bonds and the transfer of bonds would be greatly facilitated. In 1980, a law to this effect was enacted whereby Vædipapircentralen (the Danish Securities Centre) was created. All bonds quoted on the Copenhagen Stock Exchange were transferred to the system over Easter 1983. Shares listed on the Copenhagen Stock Exchange were transferred in 1988.

The electronic registration of all listed securities made it natural for the trading on the Copenhagen Stock Exchange also to be computerized. This was one of the aims of the stock-exchange reform enacted in 1986. Another part of the stock-exchange reform was the liberalization of access to the Stock Exchange. Earlier authorizations to trade on the Copenhagen Stock Exchange were granted by the Ministry of Industry. Membership was personal and hence companies such as banks, insurance companies, etc. were excluded from dealing direct on the Stock Exchange. The stock-exchange reform introduced a new kind of financial institution: a stockbroker company. Authorization to set up a stockbroker company is now granted by the Danish Supervision of Banking, Insurance and Securities and hence the earlier stockbroker monopoly has been broken. Banks, insurance companies and foreign companies are allowed to own — and indeed have set up — stockbroker companies.

Only stockbroker companies and the National Bank are allowed to trade securities on the Copenhagen Stock Exchange. However, banks, savings banks, credit institutes with a special authorization, and mortgage credit institutions, together with stockbroker companies (and the Nationalbank), are recognized in the Danish Securities Centre as stock operators, i.e. they can transfer securities from one account to another.

The Danish Securities Centre is only allowed to transfer the securities from one account to another when the stock operator holding the account which shall be debited has specifically authorized it. Private individuals cannot order such transfers directly via the Securities Centre; such transfers have to take place via the stock operator holding their account.

One of the distinguishing features of the Danish securities market is the unified clearing and settlement system of security trade operated by the Nationalbank and the Danish Securities Centre in cooperation. The central bank keeps monetary settlement accounts for stockbroker companies and credit institutions with a special authorization. As far as banks and savings banks are concerned, their regular current account at the Nationalbank also serves as a settlement account. The Nationalbank makes sure that those institutions who, on a particular day, are net buyers of securities have sufficient cash available so that settlement and clearing can be effected. The Nationalbank does not issue guarantees or grant credit for its own account in connection with operating the clearing and settlement system of trade in securities. Hence, stockbroker companies are not allowed to overdraw their accounts in the Nationalbank unless they have provided a satisfactory guarantee. Banks and savings banks can overdraw their accounts during a trading day, but they are required to keep such drawings below the ceiling fixed by the general rules for banks' access to the central bank at the end of each trading day.

The actual transfer of securities in the settlement process takes place via the security dealers' accounts with the Securities Centre. The usual settlement period is three days.

On 23 February 1989, the Copenhagen Bourse completed its switch to electronic dealings. The introduction of the electronic system made Copenhagen one of the most modern and technically advanced bourses in the world for bonds, shares, options and futures dealing, marking the end of the monopoly held by 27 stock brokerages.

Rationalization threatens stockbrokers, with small family firms finding it hard to compete with banks' broking units, particularly since the October 1987 crash reduced turnover and computerized trading pushed up costs. This has given rise to speculation that the number of Danish brokers could drop dramatically.

All securities have been electronically traded since the first quarter of 1989. Trading is based on a matching system which brings buy-and-sell orders together at market clearing prices and the acceptance system which allows buyers and sellers to be more specific on their requirements. Requirements for reporting are automatically fulfilled by the electronic system and trades outside the system must be reported after the deal has been made.

In December 1989, Denmark's Futures and Options Guarantee Fund (FUTOP) launched three- and six-month futures contracts on the Copenhagen Stock Exchange's new 250-share index (the KFX index). The index is calculated every five minutes on the central trading and information system of the exchange. The contracts are traded in multiples of DKR 100 000. Nine-month futures, plus put-and-call options on the futures, are planned when the market becomes sufficiently liquid. Most trading so far has been in three-month contracts.

In the context of closer cooperation between European stock exchanges, Copenhagen sees itself as a bridge between the European Community and the Nordic countries. During 1989 major progress was made in the exchange of trading information among the Nordic exchanges, with agreement reached between the Oslo, Helsinki, Stockholm and Copenhagen Stock Exchanges on an inter-Scandinavian stock-exchange network dubbed Nordix.

Within the European Community stock-exchange cooperation, it was agreed to establish a joint information system with the working title PIPE, which, it is hoped, will eventually be linked to Nordix.

As far as developments on the stock market in 1992 were concerned, the bond and equities markets have failed to recover significantly from the shock imparted by the rejection of the EMU Treaty in June. The medium-term outlook is adversely affected by currency depreciations in important export markets as well as sluggishness elsewhere. Thus the all-share index has fallen by over 20% since January 1992 (see Graph 32), making Copenhagen the most badly hit exchange in Europe.

A number of developments have taken place during 1992 which make the Copenhagen market more attractive. Fees

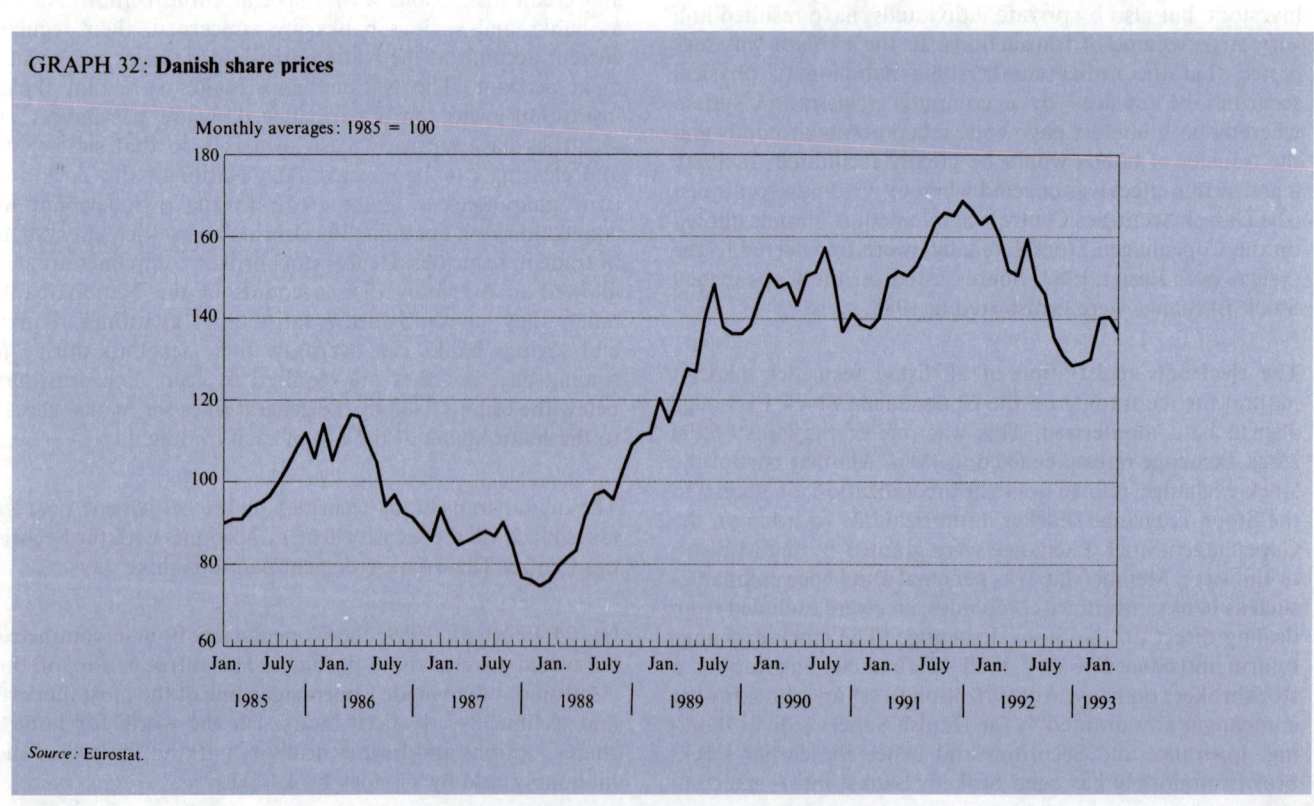

GRAPH 32: **Danish share prices**

Monthly averages: 1985 = 100

Source: Eurostat.

to market makers were reduced three times in 1992, finally being abolished from the beginning of January 1993. Contracts concluded on the futures and options market increased by 50% in 1992 and options on three new shares were introduced in January 1993 in addition to the options trading that already exists on five shares (including the two main banks). In autumn 1992 trading was introduced for international securities which are not listed on the main exchange, with turnover on some of the Nordic shares listed being from 20 to 70% of that on the domestic markets of these shares.

4.2. Sector-specific issues

4.2.1. The Danish financial sector and Scandinavian difficulties

The troubles affecting many of Scandinavia's financial institutions, including bail-outs in Norway, Finland and Sweden, have raised investor questions about the soundness of Danish institutions. The global slowdown in economic expansion and the stagnation in consumer expenditure are factors affecting all financial institutions, regional or global. In addition, problems in the real-estate sector world-wide have stretched most financial institutions. However, the geographical proximity of problems with comparable financial institutions should not be used to infer that the specific Scandinavian disease also applies in Denmark. Thus Danish banks appear to be in far better shape than their Nordic counterparts. They have survived falling asset prices, a long economic stagnation and larger bad-debt provisions (see Graph 33), mainly because they are better capitalized than their neighbours but also because of closer supervision, with a focus on the liabilities side of the balance sheet and the inclusion of guarantees, and earlier liberalization in the cycle. Danish financial institutions are among the least loaned-up financial systems. However, since the early 1980s interest margins (see Table 15), which give an insight into pressures on the asset quality of a bank's portfolio, have narrowed. This is not unusual as international competition has increased and financial disintermediation spread, with the result that banks have had to reduce their lending rates and fees on services to keep business. The margin is obviously affected by the structure of business, since domestic spreads are generally wider than those of international or wholesale operations. Another factor behind lower margins has been the large securities portfolios of the banks, with about 20% of balance sheets invested in bonds and shares and a large proportion of assets in cash and bank balances. Danish

banks stand to benefit on the interest margins side from tighter international capital requirements. Denmark's largest banks, in particular Danske, Unibank, Bikuben and Jyske Bank, remain strongly capitalized although in the case of Danske, which recently had to pump DKR 2,5 billion into Baltica Holdings, which controls the country's biggest insurance group, to acquire a 32% equity stake, and Unibank, where a deficit of DKR 4,5 billion in 1992 mainly resulted from currency market losses and depreciation charges, after losses of DKR 1,7 billion in 1991, have eroded their capital bases. In November, Unibank raised DKR 3,3 billion in supplementary capital, 1,3 billion of which was subscribed by the bank's customers, the remainder from institutional investors. Even though the banks' capital base was eroded to some extent, total supplementary capital to the tune of DKR 13 billion was raised last year after 6 billion in 1991. When rules for capital adequacy were applied to Danish banks, it was found that their average capital ratio was almost 14%. The banks are not, therefore, faced with the difficulty of strengthening their capital ratios in a period of economic sluggishness. Minimum capital ratios were fixed at 10% coming down to 9% from 1 January 1993 and 8% in 1995, although this will be counterbalanced by a reduction (to 20% in 1993 and 1994 and 10% from 1995) in the share of subordinated loan capital which can be counted in the capital base.

If interest margins cannot be widened substantially, the other main element in improving profitability is a reduction in operating expenditure. Here, Danish banks have, in the past, tended to be lifetime employers with generous salaries and traditional bonuses. Employment in the banking sector reached a peak in 1987 (Table 15) and the number of branches has fallen significantly between 1985 and 1990 (see Table 13). The merger activities in 1989-90 will further emphasize rationalization with the two big banks cutting further branches, staff numbers, overlapping operations and subsidiaries and turning the banks into trimmer, more efficient institutions. Thus there would appear to be some margin for a contribution of lower operating costs to pre-tax profits which have been decreasing since 1989. In 1992 there were three small bank failures. However, depositors were bailed out by the deposit guarantee fund. It should be noted that interest earned in the year by the fund more than covered the rescues. The only casualty recently in the banking sector has been that of Varda Bank, the 10th ranking Danish bank based in Jutland, which in November experienced difficulties. A consortium of eight banks, including the Nationalbank put together a safety net, the first time since 1984 that such a course of action was necessary, to support the bank while restructuring operations were adopted. It was not subsequently necessary to have recourse to the safety net.

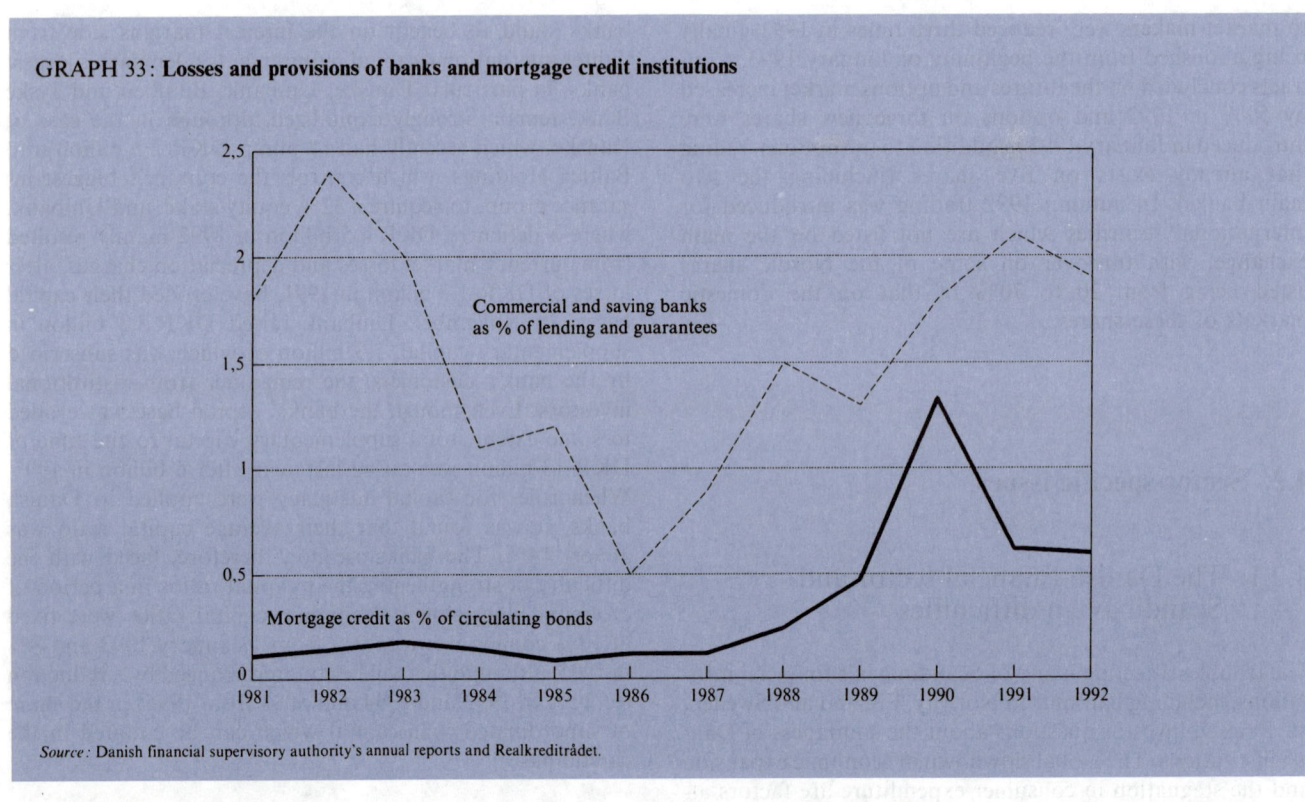

GRAPH 33: **Losses and provisions of banks and mortgage credit institutions**

Commercial and saving banks
as % of lending and guarantees

Mortgage credit as % of circulating bonds

Source: Danish financial supervisory authority's annual reports and Realkreditrådet.

Table 15

Key figures for commercial and major savings banks in Denmark

	1981	1982	1983	1984	1985	1986	1987	1988	1989	1990	1991[1]	1992[2]
Lending as % of GDP	33,5	32,2	33,8	37,0	43,8	51,3	55,8	56,1	59,3	62,0	60,9	58,0
Net profit before tax on equity in %[3]	4,3	7,8	1,9	5,3	1,2	9,9	5,2	5,5	6,7	5,1	4,8	3,1
Interest margin (%)	6,5	6,2	5,1	4,9	4,3	4,0	4,3	4,4	4,4	4,3	4,2	:
Full-time employees (thousands)	42,8	42,4	42,4	44,3	46,3	49,7	51,8	50,8	50,0	49,5	:	:

[1] Changed reporting year.
[2] First half of year.
[3] Calculated assuming average provisions and excluding value adjustment of security portfolios (see Bartholdy Nationalbank, August 1991).
Source: Danish financial authority's annual report and Realkreditrådet for mortgage credit institutions in 1991.

As far as the Danish mortgage institutions are concerned, the fundamental difference with banks is that they are not deposit-taking institutions, being funded entirely with bonds and bound by 'matching principles' that limit their interest rate, maturity and currency risks. Their margins are low, averaging less than 1%, but this is not surprising given their concentration generally on residential property and the lower risk attached to the debt. Other operating income comes primarily from service fees. Pricing for services has recently been used to boost profitability because of capital requirements. Costs are typically low since they do not operate branch networks on a scale similar to the banks. Joint ventures and purchases of real-estate agents have recently been used to increase their presence in the local market place. After years of rapid loan growth and property prices, when mortgages were granted solely on collateral without taking account of credit standing, the sharp downturn in the real-estate sector led to a sharp increase in loss provisions of the mortgage institutions as the companies found themselves in possession of more real estate with prices below original valuation. Published figures (see Table 16) are, however, inflated by tougher accounting standards in 1990 requiring provisions for expected future losses in addition to actual losses. In addition, since asset quality distress in the housing market tends to peak in the initial period after purchase and more realistic expectations on the housing market by purchasers and a more cautious approach by lenders has been in evidence now for several years, it may be that the high point of loss provisions has already been passed.

The sector which has been most badly hit in Denmark has been that of insurance. While the basic insurance operations have been profitable, difficulties have been experienced at holding company level with ambitious expansion plans. The upheaval in insurance has stemmed from the difficulties in the Scandinavian property and equities market. The knock-on effects here have been emphasized by attempts in 1991 to form a big Scandinavian financial conglomerate. Thus Uni Storebrand (formed from a merger in 1990) of Norway and Denmark's Hafnia holding company tried to take over or merge with Skandia of Sweden and Baltica of Denmark. Neither company was prepared to link with their smaller rivals and subsequent falls in their share prices led to significant investment losses in the stakes held by the predators. By acquiring such a big combined stake in Skandia, Hafnia and Uni Storebrand became increasingly dependent on the region's insurance market, both as investors and insurers. At the end of 1991, Hafnia's investments in Skandia and Baltica were almost double its own shareholders equity. Although a complex financial deal was agreed in April 1992, it fell through when Hafnia's shareholders objected to the imposition of Swedish control. A subsequent recapitalization of Hafnia, through a DKR 2 billion rights issue, was wiped out as share prices continued to fall. In August 1992, both Hafnia and Uni Storebrand were forced to suspend payment to creditors. The Hafnia holding companies assets were transferred to a new holding company leaving the debt in the former company (which is in the hands of receivers) with three Danish banks (Den Danske (DKR 1,2 billion), Bikuben (DKR 600 million) and Unidanmark (450 million)) as the largest creditors while Uni was aided by Norway's central bank. The slide in the position of Baltica was less dramatic although equity capital was halved last year following losses by its bank, write-downs on property investments in Gibraltar (recently sold) and Denmark and a fall in the value of its securities portfolio. Basic insurance business was, however, profitable and Den Danske Bank pumped DKR 2,5 billion into Baltica Holdings in return for a 32% equity stake in Baltica Insurance. In March 1993, Codan (owned by the UK Sun Alliance Group) acquired the banking, insurance, property and three other subsidiaries of Hafnia Holdings. The combined operations of Codan and Haf-

Table 16

Losses and provisions of banks and mortgage credit institutions

	1981	1982	1983	1984	1985	1986	1987	1988	1989	1990	1991	1992[1]
Commercial and savings banks as % of lending and guarantees	1,8	2,4	2,0	1,1	1,2	0,5	0,9	1,5	1,3	1,8	2,1	1,9
Mortgage credit institutions as % of circulating bonds[2]	0,11	0,14	0,18	0,14	0,09	0,12	0,12	0,24	0,47	1,33	0,62	0,60

[1] First half year.
[2] Until 1984, realized losses. From 1984 to 1989 inclusive, realized losses and provisions to cover expected losses from redeemed, but not yet sold mortgage. From 1990, provisions must cover all expected losses. Realized losses in 1990 were 0,51%.

Source: Danish financial authority's annual report and Realkreditrådet for mortgage credit institutions in 1991.

nia will constitute the largest general business insurer in Denmark and it will have about 12% of the life insurance market.

Thus a certain Scandinavian link does exist through the insurance companies to the banking system but it is misleading to assume that these difficulties automatically apply to Denmark because of its location and the problems at holding company level. Graph 34 shows how country risk ratings have evolved favourably in the Danish case *vis-à-vis* its neighbours.

4.2.2. Employment contribution

The main section of this paper looks to the services sector for increased employment opportunities in Denmark. However, given the sluggishness of output in the financial sector (Graph 35) by Community standards, the situation is not such as to provide this employment response. In fact the situation is the opposite. The adjustments in the financial sector to meet changed conditions have resulted in very considerable staff reductions; on the basis of output and

employment data in the financial sector (Graph 36) some further cutbacks seem indicated. Overall in the financial sector about 6 000 jobs have so far been lost as part of the adjustment process. In addition, the second largest bank, Unibank, has announced that it will reduce its staff by 1 700 (or about 15%) by 1994. At the time of its merger, Unibank had 12 940 employees in 798 branches. By the end of 1992, there were 11 576 employees in 480 branches. Although exact figures are not available for Den Danske Bank, it is likely that trends are similar. In the insurance sector there have also been notable increases in redundancies. Thus in February 1992, Topdanmark reduced its staff by 600, in August 1992 Hafnia announced the dismissal of 524 employees or about one fifth of total staff in Denmark, Baltica will release 10% of its staff (400 employees) over the near future while other companies have also shed labour — Kgl. Brand (94), Alm. Brand (80), Zurich (46) and Codan (40).

It would therefore seem that any employment response in the next couple of years in the financial sector will be negative, with companies intent on rationalizing, reducing operating expenditure and concentrating on their core activities, rather than taking on additional staff.

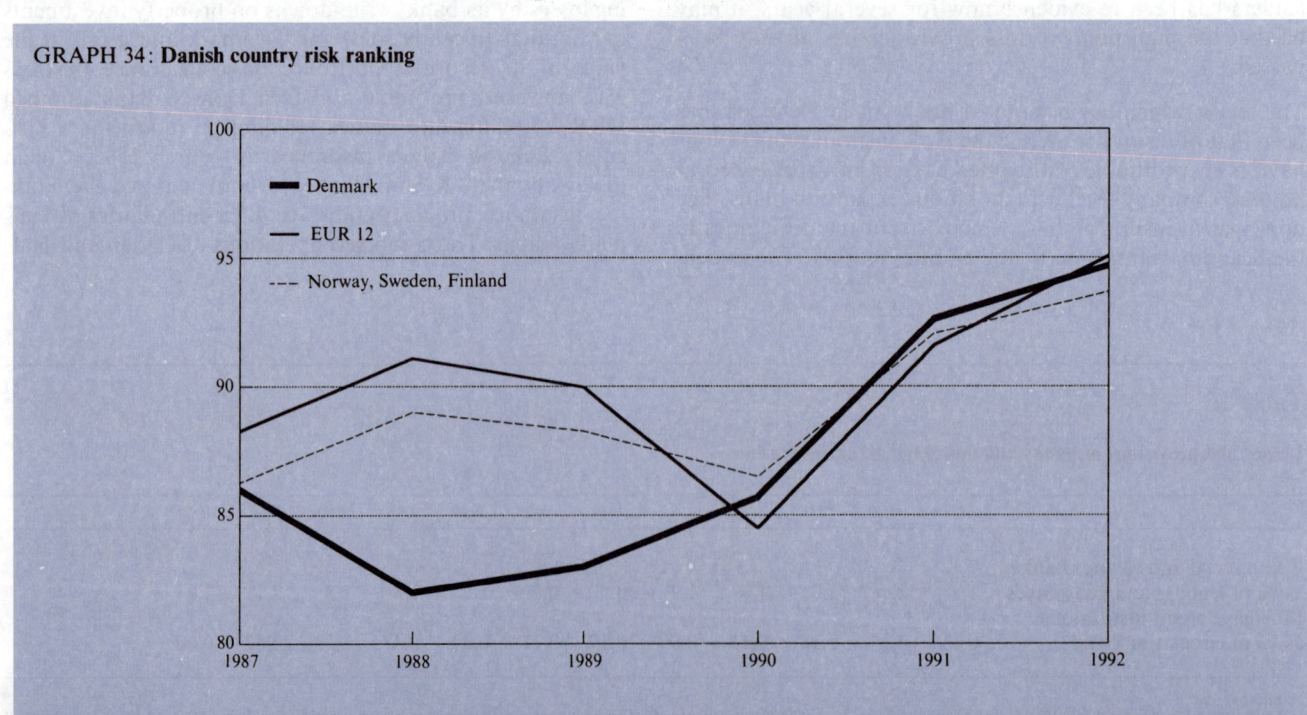

GRAPH 34: **Danish country risk ranking**

Source: Euromoney, based on political risk (20%), debt risk (20%), economic indicators (10%), credit indicators (10%), other market indicators (40%). A perfect score is 100. In 1992, country risks ranged from Japan (99,6) to Cambodia (2,6). Weighted by GDP averages for EUR 12 and Nordic countries.

GRAPH 35: **Volume of output in NACE 69A in 1990**

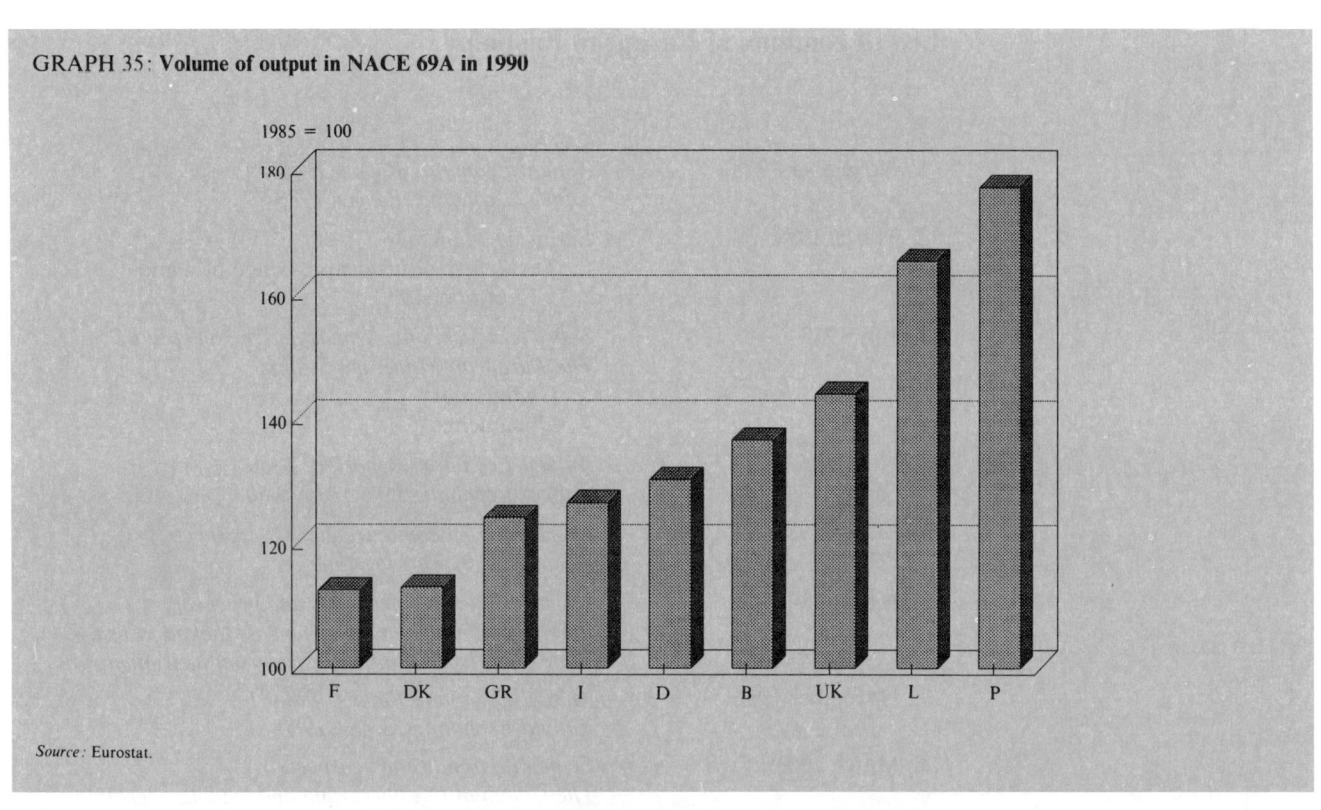

Source: Eurostat.

GRAPH 36: **Evolution of employment and output in NACE 69A sector**

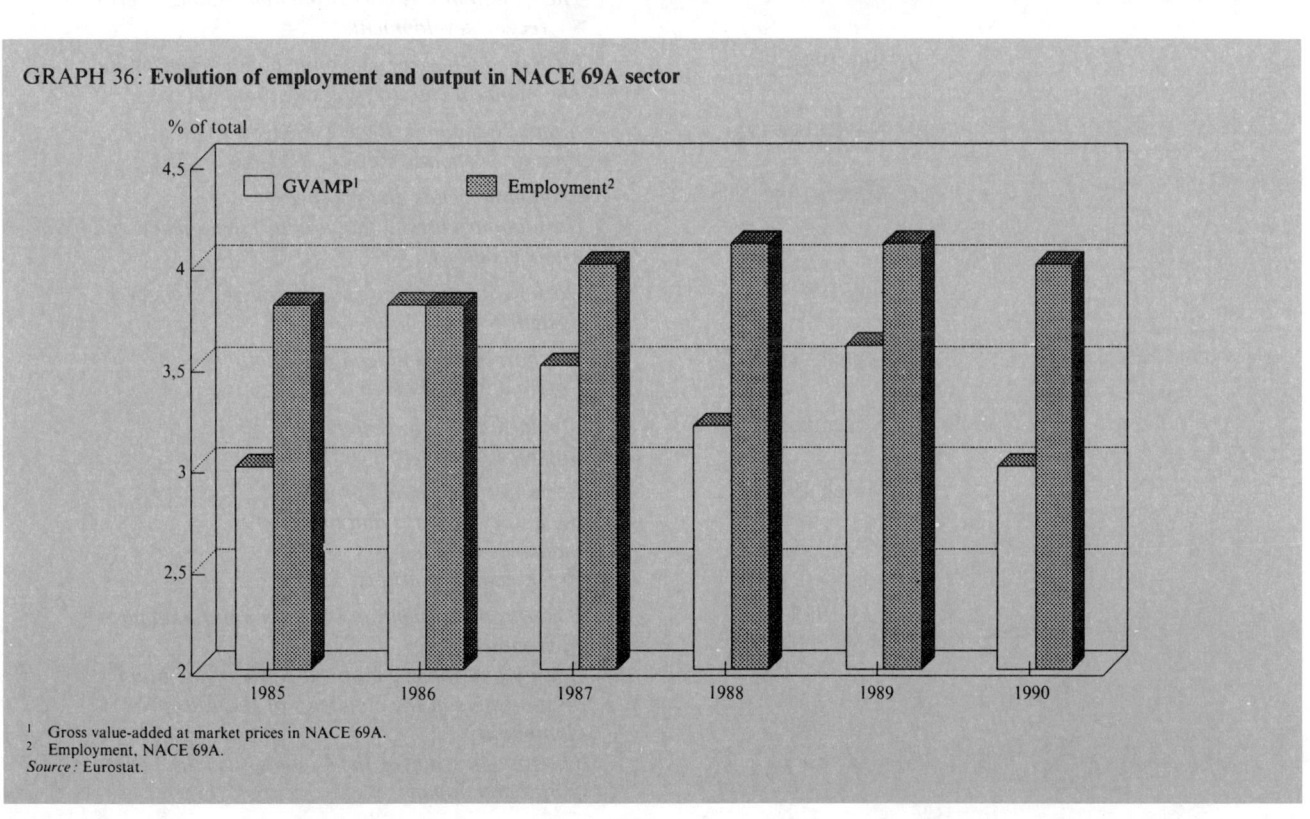

[1] Gross value-added at market prices in NACE 69A.
[2] Employment, NACE 69A.
Source: Eurostat.

List of contents of European Economy

17, September 1983	— *The borrowing and lending activities of the Community in 1982*
18, November 1983	— *Annual Economic Report 1983-84* — *Annual Economic Review 1983-84*
19, March 1984	— *Economic trends and prospects* — *Industrial labour costs* — *Medium-term budget balance and the public debt* — *The issue of protectionism*
20, July 1984	— *Some aspects of industrial productive performance in the European Community: an appraisal* — *Profitability, relative factor prices and capital/labour substitution in the Community, the United States and Japan, 1960-83* — *Convergence and coordination of macroeconomic policies: some basic issues*
21, September 1984	— *Commission report to the Council and to Parliament on the borrowing and lending activities of the Community in 1983*
22, November 1984	— *Annual Economic Report 1984-85* — *Annual Economic Review 1984-85*
23, March 1985	— *Economic trends and prospects 1984-85*
24, July 1985	— *The borrowing and lending activities of the Community in 1984*
25, September 1985	— *Competitiveness of European industry: situation to date* — *The determinants of supply in industry in the Community* — *The development of market services in the European Community, the United States and Japan* — *Technical progress, structural change and employment*
26, November 1985	— *Annual Economic Report 1985-86* — *Annual Economic Review 1985-86*
27, March 1986	— *Employment problems: views of businessmen and the workforce* — *Compact — A prototype macroeconomic model of the European Community in the world economy*
28, May 1986	— *Commission report to the Council and to Parliament on the borrowing and lending activities of the Community in 1985*
29, July 1986	— *Annual Economic Review 1986-87*
30, November 1986	— *Annual Economic Report 1986-87*
31, March 1987	— *The determinants of investment* — *Estimation and simulation of international trade linkages in the Quest model*
32, May 1987	— *Commission report to the Council and to Parliament on the borrowing and lending activities of the Community in 1986*

Special editions

Special issue 1979	— *Changes in industrial structure in the European economies since the oil crisis 1973-78*
	— *Europe — its capacity to change in question!*
Special edition 1990	— *The impact of the internal market by industrial sector: the challenge for the Member States*
Special edition No 1/91	— *The economics of EMU*
Special edition No 2/91	— *The path of reform in Central and Eastern Europe*
Special edition No 1/92	— *The economics of limiting CO_2 emissions*

Reports and studies

1-1993	— *The economic and financial situation in Italy*
2-1993	— *Shaping a market economy legal system*
3-1993	— *Market services and European integration: the challenges for the 1990s*
4-1993	— *The economic and financial situation in Belgium*
5-1993	— *The economic of Community public finance (in preparation)*

Europe

THE STRANGE SUPERPOWER

David Buchan

The European Community has developed into a curious creature. It has solid legs built on economic power, trade, aid and, maybe one day, a common currency. But its decentralized nature gives it a political hydra for a head.

This book tackles the contrast between the Community's growing world role and its persistent inability to play this part as a conventional superpower would — a paradox that is eased, yet not resolved, by the Maastricht Treaty. The book argues that, in a world shaped by and for nation States, the Community will forever remain a strange superpower, but that for all the apparent muddle of its institutions and occasional serious mistakes of its policies, it has gained a regional and global role from which it cannot now shrink back.

181 pp. Price: ECU 22 (excluding VAT)
CM-78-93-976-EN-C

This work retraces the history of the High Authority of the European Coal and Steel Community from its creation, following the Schuman Declaration of 9 May 1950, to the implementation of the Merger Treaty, which established a single Council and Commission for the three European Communities (ECSC, EEC and Euratom) in 1967.

The ECSC's founders hoped not only to create a common market between the Member States, but also to bridge the divide between former enemies and foster a new political climate. The brainchild of two convinced Europeans, Jean Monnet and Robert Schuman, the ECSC was bold in providing the initial momentum for European integration. It was to be an arduous task, one which confronted the High Authority with numerous difficulties. The authors describe how this supranational body coped with the complex problems posed by political and economic events, and with the highs and lows of European integration. In many areas, the High Authority was both pioneer and role-model.

This book is addressed to those who remember the years of hope which followed the Second World War, and to future generations who will be called upon to lead Europe in the 21st century.

Its authors are Dirk Spierenburg, the Netherlands' principal negotiator of the Treaty of Paris, Member of the High Authority for 10 years and its Vice-President from 1958 to 1962, and Professor Raymond Poidevin of the University of Strasbourg III, author of a biography of Robert Schuman and an expert on the early years of the Communities.

This publication is available in the following language:

French: **HISTOIRE DE LA HAUTE AUTORITÉ DE LA COMMUNAUTÉ EUROPÉENNE DU CHARBON ET DE L'ACIER**
Bruylant — Bruxelles, 1993 ● Price: ECU 87.50

Sales: Office for Official Publications of the European Communities, L-2985 Luxembourg; and accredited sales agents in the Member States.
CM-77-92-449-FR-C

This book by Giovanni Grasso, lecturer in criminal law at the University of Catania, deals with the relationship between Community rules and the criminal law systems of the Member States.

While the general view is that criminal law does not fall within the terms of reference of the European Communities but is the preserve of each Member State, the many ways in which Community legislation influences national criminal law cannot be overlooked.

For one thing, Community legislation has a direct impact on rules governing penalties in that it can take the form of punitive measures (not necessarily in the criminal courts) designed to secure the protection of legal interests generated by the activities of the European Communities.

For another, it has indirect effects on national criminal law, in particular by narrowing the scope of Member States' criminal law, but also by defining the types and severity of penalties in certain situations.

How does Community law influence the rules providing for penalties imposed to secure the legal interests of the European Communities?

What 'protection models' potentially exist for the interests of the European Communities, as determined mainly by Community provisions, by the widening of the scope of national criminal provisions and by measures to harmonize and coordinate the criminal laws of the Member States?

What effects does Community law already have on the criminal law systems of the Member States?

These are some of the questions raised in this book, which takes the form of an exhaustive examination of the relationship between Community law and the criminal law systems of the Member States and is one of the rare attempts to put the matter into an orderly theoretical perspective.

This publication is available in the following language:

Spanish: **COMUNIDADES EUROPEAS Y DERECHO PENAL**
Ediciones de la Universidad de Castilla-La Mancha, 1993 • Price: ECU 21.80

Sales: Office for Official Publications of the European Communities,
L-2985 Luxembourg; and accredited sales agents in the Member States.
CM-75-92-308-ES-C

Eastern Europe and the USSR

THE CHALLENGE OF FREEDOM

GILES MERRITT

The sparks of unrest that leapt from Berlin in November 1989 to Moscow's Red Square in August 1991 are firing an explosion of political and economic change. Out of the ashes of Communism is emerging the shape of a vast new European market-place stretching from the Atlantic to the Pacific.

In his fascinating account of Europe's fast-changing East-West relationships, Giles Merritt argues that a massive rescue operation must be mounted to ensure the success of these changes. The upheaval of Communism's collapse is 'The challenge of freedom'.

Written with the cooperation and support of the European Commission, this book sets out to identify the key policy areas where a new partnership is being forged between the countries of Eastern and Western Europe. It offers a privileged insight into the current thinking of European Community officials, politicians and industrial leaders, and analyses the factors that will determine whether the emerging market economies of Eastern Europe can truly be absorbed into a single European economy.

Immensely readable and often disturbing, this important book contains much up-to-date and hitherto unpublished information on such major East-West problem areas as energy, environmental control, immigration, trade relations, agriculture and investment. It also examines the arguments surrounding a 'Marshall Plan' for Eastern Europe that would emulate the famous US aid programme that helped relaunch the economies of Western Europe in the aftermath of World War II.

For anyone concerned about the future of Eastern Europe and the USSR, whether from a political, social or economic standpoint, this book is essential reading.

256 pp. — Price: ECU 14.30 *(excluding VAT)*
CM-71-91-655-EN-C

Bulletin
of the European
Communities

The *Bulletin of the European Communities*, published by the Commission as a complement to the General Report, is the only official reference work containing a month-by-month account of Community activities.

Produced in the nine official languages of the Community, the Bulletin is a user-friendly and reliable reference tool thanks to:

- its clear presentation of the different stages of Community legislation, with copious references to the Official Journal and to previous issues;

- its monthly and annual indexes;

- its subject-based structure providing easy access to topical information on areas of special interest: the single market, economic and social cohesion, the Community's role in the world, etc.;

- its documentation section, which often includes previously unpublished material, such as addresses to the UN General Assembly, G7 declarations, etc.

Supplements to the Bulletin are published from time to time, containing background material on significant Community issues of the day. These are included in the annual subscription.

The following annual reports are also published in the nine official languages of the Community:

The **General Report on the Activities of the European Communities** is the most compact and comprehensive source book on the Community's progress over the years. It gives a bird's-eye view of matters handled at Community level, highlights the different phases of the decision-making process and serves as a guide to the intricacies of Community legislation, which reflect the economic and political challenges facing Europe.

The **Agricultural Situation in the Community** sets out the main policy decisions, traces developments in the most important markets and looks at the other aspects of the agricultural situation. It includes a detailed statistical annex.

The **Report on Competition Policy** gives a general view of the application of competition policy over the previous year. It is divided into four parts: main developments, policy towards enterprises, State intervention, and contacts with Community and other institutions.

INFO92

The Community database focusing on the objectives and the social dimension of the single market

As a practical guide to the single market, INFO92 contains vital information for all those determined to be ready for 1992.

INFO92 is really a simple market scoreboard, recording the state of play on the stage-by-stage progress of Commission proposals up to their adoption by the Council, summarizing each notable development and placing it in context, and keeping track of the transposition of directives into Member States' national legislation.

Using INFO92 is simplicity itself. It can be consulted on-screen by means of a wide range of everyday equipment connected to specialized data-relay networks. Fast transmission, the virtually instant updating facility (several times a day, if necessary) and dialogue procedures requiring no prior training make INFO92 ideal for the general public as well as for business circles and the professions.

The system offers easy access to information thanks to the choice of menus available and to the logical presentation modelled on the structure of the *White Paper*, the *Social Charter* and the decision-making process within the institutions.

Enquiries may also be made to the Commission Offices in the Member States or – for small businesses – the Euro-Info Centres now open in all regions of the Community.

Eurobases Helpdesk $\left\{ \begin{array}{l} \text{Tel.}: \quad \text{(32-2) 295 00 03} \\ \text{Fax}: \quad \text{(32-2) 296 06 24} \end{array} \right.$

22/10/93

DIRECTORY

OF COMMUNITY LEGISLATION IN FORCE
and other acts of the Community institutions

The Community's legal system is of direct concern to the individual citizen as much as to the Member States themselves.

Both lawyers and non-lawyers, then, need to be familiar not just with national law, but also with Community legislation, which is implemented, applied or interpreted by national law and in some cases takes precedence over it.

To make Community legislation more accessible to the public, the Commission of the European Communities publishes a Directory, updated twice a year, covering:

- binding instruments of secondary legislation arising out of the Treaties establishing the three Communities (regulations, decisions, directives, etc.);
- other legislation (internal agreements, etc.);
- agreements between the Communities and non-member countries.

Each entry in the Directory gives the number and title of the instrument, together with a reference to the Official Journal in which it is to be found. Any amending instruments are also indicated, with the appropriate references in each case.

The legislation is classified by subject matter. Instruments classifiable in more than one subject area appear under each of the headings concerned.

The Directory proper (Vol. I) is accompanied by two indexes (Vol. II), one chronological by document number and the other alphabetical by keyword.

The Directory is available in the nine official languages of the Community.

Official Journal
of the European Communities

DIRECTORY
OF COMMUNITY
LEGISLATION IN FORCE
and other acts
of the Community institutions

1 064 pp. – ECU 83
ISBN 92-77-77093-7 (Volume I)
ISBN 92-77-77094-5 (Volume II)
ISBN 92-77-77095-3 (Volume I and II)
FX-86-91-001-EN-C
FX-86-91-002-EN-C

EUROPEAN ECONOMY

European Economy appears four times a year, in March, May, July and November. It contains important reports and communications from the Commission to the Council and to Parliament on the economic situation and developments, as well as on the borrowing and lending activities of the Community. In addition, *European Economy* presents reports and studies on problems concerning economic policy.

Two supplements accompany the main periodical:

– Series A – 'Economic trends' appears monthly except in August and describes with the aid of tables and graphs the most recent trends of industrial production, consumer prices, unemployment, the balance of trade, exchange rates, and other indicators. This supplement also presents the Commission staff's macroeconomic forecasts and Commission communications to the Council on economic policy.

– Series B – 'Business and consumer survey results' gives the main results of opinion surveys of industrial chief executives (orders, stocks, production outlook, etc.) and of consumers (economic and financial situation and outlook, etc.) in the Community, and other business cycle indicators. It also appears monthly, with the exception of August.

Unless otherwise indicated, the texts are published under the responsibility of the Directorate-General for Economic and Financial Affairs of the Commission of the European Communities, 200 rue de la Loi, B-1049 Brussels, to which enquiries other than those related to sales and subscriptions should be addressed.

Subscription terms are shown on the back cover and the addresses of the sales offices are shown on the third page of the cover.

Success in business

depends on the decisions you make ... which depend on the information you receive

Make sure that your decisions are based on information that is accurate and complete!

In a period of rapid adjustment, with national economies merging into a single European economy under the impetus of 1992, reliable information on the performance of specialized industry sectors is essential to suppliers, customers, bankers and policy-makers.

Small and medium-sized enterprises, in particular, need easy access to information.

The market must be defined, measured and recorded. Information is needed on production capacities, bottlenecks, future developments, etc.

Panorama of EC industry 93

An extensive review of the situation and outlook of the manufacturing and service industries in the European Community

1 176 pp.   Price: ECU 125
ISBN 92-826-5428-1 * CO-76-92-625-EN-C

SOCIAL EUROPE

Social Europe, published by the Commission of the European Communities, Directorate-General for Employment, Industrial Relations and Social Affairs (DG V), Coordination and Information Policy Unit, deals with current social affairs in Europe.

The basic review appears three times a year. In addition, a number of supplements/files are published annually, each dealing in depth with a given subject.

OFFICE FOR OFFICIAL PUBLICATIONS OF THE EUROPEAN COMMUNITIES
2, rue Mercier — L-2985 Luxembourg [Tel. (352) 499 28-1]

ENERGY

A CHALLENGE FOR EUROPE AND THE WORLD

Since it first appeared in 1985 **Energy in Europe** has become recognized as an invaluable source of information on both the policy-making and the operational aspects of European Community energy policy. Subscribers include leaders of energy-consuming and energy-producing industries and other decision-makers in the private and public sectors, as well as major consultancies and research institutes in and outside the Community.

In the present situation within the Community, itself at the eve of the single market, and *vis-à-vis* the huge energy problems, as well as the potential, of our neighbours in Central and Eastern Europe and in the Commonwealth of Independent States, the energy sector is of the greatest strategic importance. An understanding of it is indispensable in many areas of economic activity. It also constitutes a crucial factor within a debate of truly global importance, namely the protection of the environment, including the global warming issue.

Energy in Europe continues to keep its readers abreast of the ongoing situation as regards overall policy, markets, energy planning, and the constant quest for cleaner and more efficient energy technology.

Market trends and perspectives are covered in **two regular issues** each year, and also in a **Short-term energy outlook** appearing in the first half of the year and an **Annual energy review** at the end of the year which includes the world energy situation by region including EC Member States, the short-term energy outlook for the Community, and a review of trends in main indicators over 10 years. Further **Special Issues** are also produced in connection with major developments or events, including international conferences on or relevant to the energy sector.

Energy in Europe appears in English but each issue also contains translations into French, German or Spanish of articles from the preceding issue.

22/10/93

Also available:

Treaty on European Union

253 pp. * ECU 9 * ISBN 92-824-0959-7 * RX-73-92-796-EN-C — 1992

Conradh ar an Aontas Eorpach

253 pp. * ECU 9 * ISBN 92-824-0964-3 * RX-73-92-796-GA-C — 1992

National implementing measures to give effect to the White Paper of the Commission on the completion of the internal market – *Situation at 30 April 1993*

570 pp. * ECU 40 * ISBN 92-826-5368-4 * CM-78-93-677-EN-C — 1993

Adaptation of remuneration systems

75 pp. * ECU 11.50 * ISBN 92-826-5640-3 * CE-78-93-176-EN-C — 1993

The geographical dimension of competition in the European single market

182 pp. * ECU 26.50 * ISBN 92-826-5613-6 * CV-78-93-136-EN-C — 1993

European Monitoring Centre for Drugs and Drug Addiction (EMCDDA) – Inventory of EC (legal) texts on drugs

1 330 pp. * ECU 101 * ISBN 92-826-5415-X * CM-76-92-722-EN-C — 1993

Reports of Commission Decisions relating to competition – 1989/1990

247 pp. * ECU 12 * ISBN 92-826-3868-5 * CV-73-92-772-EN-C — 1992

Harmonization of company law in the European Community – Measures adopted and proposed – *Situation as at 1 March 1992*

518 pp. * ECU 54 * ISBN 92-826-4314-X * C1-74-92-831-EN-C — 1992

The European Community and human rights

61 pp. * ECU 8 * ISBN 92-826-5083-9 * CM-76-92-407-EN-C — 1993·

The opening-up of public procurement

46 pp. * ECU 6 * ISBN 92-826-5130-4 * CO-77-92-085-EN-C — 1993

Enterprise and people aspects in the information technology sector to the year 2000 – *Social Europe – Supplement 2/92*

111 pp. * ECU 9 * ISBN 92-826-4537-1 * CE-NC-92-002-EN-C — 1992

The regulation of working conditions in the Member States of the European Community – Volume 1 – *Social Europe – Supplement 4/92*

114 pp. * ECU 9 * ISBN 92-826-4996-2 * CE-NC-92-004-EN-C — 1992

XXVIth General Report on the Activities of the European Communities – 1992

520 pp. * ECU 20 * ISBN 92-826-5340-4 * CM-76-92-681-EN-C — 1993

EUR 14006 – Thesaurus guide – *Second edition, prepared by EUROBrokerS*

1033 pp. * ECU 78 * ISBN 92-826-4956-3 * CD-NA-14006-EN-C — 1993

EUR 14197 – Evaluation of economic effects: relevance and impacts of EC programmes promoting industrial R&D with special emphasis on small and medium-sized enterprises (pilot methodological study)
K. HORNSCHILD, F. MEYER-KRAHMER

129 pp. * ECU 13.50 * ISBN 92-826-3817-0 * CD-NA-14197-EN-C — 1992

EUR 14198 – Evaluation of the impact of European Community research programmes upon the competitiveness of European industry – concepts and approaches
J.S. METCALFE, L. GEORGHIOU, P. CUNNINGHAM, H.M. CAMERON

44 pp. * ECU 6.00 * ISBN 92-826-3818-9 * CD-NA-14198-EN-C — 1992

EUR 14777 – Research publications 1992

128 pp. * ECU 20 * ISBN 92-826-6165-2 * CD-NA-14777-EN-C — 1993

Employment in Europe – 1993

206 pp. * ECU 12 * ISBN 92-826-6055-9 * CE-79-93-275-EN-C — 1993

Energy policies and trends in the European Community
– Energy in Europe

197 pp. * ECU 21 * ISSN 1017-6705 * CS-BI-93-001-4H-C — 1993

Annual energy review – *Energy in Europe, Special issue, April 1993*

183 pp. * ECU 19 * ISBN 92-826-5325-0 * CS-77-92-102-EN-C — 1993

Focus on the East – *Energy in Europe*

157 pp. * ECU 19 * ISSN 1017-6705 * CS-BI-92-001-4H-C — 1992

A view to the future – *Energy in Europe*

176 pp. * ECU 19 * ISBN 92-826-3665-8 * CS-75-92-841-EN-C — 1992

Administrative structures for environmental management in the European Community

189 pp. * ECU 11 * ISBN 92-826-5152-5 * CR-77-92-134-EN-C — 1993

Small business and competition – A practical guide

55 pp. * ECU 6 * ISBN 92-826-5212-2 * CT-77-92-409-EN-C — 1993

Unemployed women in the EC – Statistical facts

103 pp. * ECU 7 * ISBN 92-826-6008-7 * CA-79-93-340-EN-C — 1993

Eurostat – European statistics: official sources

206 pp. * free of charge * ISBN 92-826-5328-5 * CA-76-92-900-3A-C — 1993

The European Community as a publisher 1993-1994 – *Extract from our publications catalogue*

160 pp. * JY-76-92-794-EN-C — 1993

The finances of Europe, Daniel STRASSER

439 pp. * ECU 18.50 * ISBN 92-826-2306-8 * CM-60-90-280-EN-C — 1992

XXIInd Report on Competition Policy – 1992

531 pp. * ECU 32 * ISBN 92-826-6126-1 * CM-76-93-689-EN-C — 1993

Europe in figures – *Third edition*

256 pp. * ECU 16.50 * ISBN 92-826-3371-1 * CA-70-91-895-EN-C — 1992

Inventory of taxes levied in the Member States of the European Communities – *14th edition*

726 pp. * ECU 80 * ISBN 92-826-0417-9 * CM-59-90-855-EN-C — 1992

A common market for services – *Current status 1 January 1993*
Banking • Insurance • Transactions in securities • Transport services • New technologies and services • Capital movements • Free movement of labour and the professions
(Internal market – Volume 1)

184 pp. * ECU 19 * ISBN 92-826-5257-2 * CO-10-93-001-EN-C — 1993

The elimination of frontier controls – *Current status 1 January 1993*
Control of goods • Control of individuals • Value-added tax • Excise duties
(Internal market – Volume 2)

128 pp. * ECU 19 * ISBN 92-826-5268-8 * CO-10-93-002-EN-C — 1993

Conditions for business cooperation – *Current status 1 January 1993*
Company law • Intellectual property • Company taxation – **Public procurement**
Internal market for energy
(Internal market – Volume 3)

104 pp. * ECU 19 * ISBN 92-826-5277-7 * CO-10-93-003-EN-C — 1993

Community social policy – *Labour market • Employment and pay • Improved living and working conditions • Free movement of workers • Social protection • Freedom of association and collective bargaining • Information, consultation and participation of employees • Equal treatment for men and women • Vocational training • Health and safety at work • Rights and protection of children and adolescents • The elderly • The disabled*
(Completing the internal market – Volume 6)

308 pp. * ECU 34 * ISBN 92-826-3609-7 * CO-62-91-006-EN-C — 1992

Address by Jacques Delors, President of the Commission, to the European Parliament on the occasion of the investiture debate of the new Commission – The Commission's work programme for 1993-94 – The Commission's legislative programme for 1993 – Joint declaration on the 1993 legislative programme – *Supplement 1/93 – Bull. EC*

69 pp. * ECU 6 * ISBN 92-826-5358-7 * CM-NF-93-001-EN-C — 1993

Research after Maastricht: an assessment, a strategy –
Supplement 2/92 – Bull. EC

49 pp. * ECU 5 * ISBN 92-826-4307-7 * CM-NF-92-002-EN-C — 1992

Europe and the challenge of enlargement – *Supplement 3/92 – Bull. EC*

24 pp. * ECU 5 * ISBN 92-826-4524-X * CM-NF-92-003-EN-C — 1992

The challenge of enlargement – Commission opinion on Austria's application for membership – *Supplement 4/92 – Bull. EC*

49 pp. * ECU 5 * ISBN 92-826-4989-X * CM-NF-92-004-EN-C — 1993

The challenge of enlargement – Commission opinion on Sweden's application for membership – *Supplement 5/92 – Bull. EC*

59 pp. * ECU 5 * ISBN 92-826-5498-2 * CM-NF-92-005-EN-C — 1993

The challenge of enlargement – Commission opinion on Finland's application for membership – *Supplement 6/92 – Bull. EC*

55 pp. * ECU 5 * ISBN 92-826-5755-8 * CM-NF-92-006-EN-C — 1993

The challenge of enlargement – Commission opinion on Norway's application for membership – *Supplement 2/93 – Bull. EC*

56 pp. * ECU 6 * ISBN 92-826-5932-1 * CM-NF-93-002-EN-C — 1993

Study on transfer of the head office of a company from one Member State to another, K.P.W.G. European Business Centre, Brussels

66 pp. * ECU 8.50 * ISBN 92-826-5882-1 * C1-79-93-017-EN-C — 1993

The creation of the internal market in insurance, Bill POOL

126 pp. * ECU 10.50 * ISBN 92-826-0246-X * CB-58-90-336-EN-C — 1992

European Economy – No 44 – One market, one money – An evaluation of the potential benefits and costs of forming an economic and monetary union

351 pp. * ECU 18 * ISSN 0379-0991 * CB-AR-90-044-EN-C — 1992

European Economy – The economics of EMU – Background studies for European Economy No 44 'One market, one money' *Special edition No 1 – 1991*

248 pp. * ECU 18 * ISBN 92-826-1996-6 * CM-60-90-208-EN-C — 1992

European Economy – No 49 – Reform issues in the former Soviet Union

240 pp. * ECU 20 * ISSN 0379-0991 * CM-AR-91-049-EN-C — 1993

European Economy – No 52 – The European Community as a world trade partner

218 pp. * ECU 23.50 * ISSN 0379-0991 * CM-AR-92-052-EN-C — 1993

European Economy – No 54 – Annual Economic Report for 1993

254 pp. * ECU 23.50 * ISSN 0379-0991 * CM-AR-92-054-EN-C — 1993

European Economy – *Reports and studies* **– The economic and financial situation in Italy – No 1/93**

175 pp. * ECU 26 * ISSN 0379-0991 * CM-78-93-944-EN-C — 1993

European Economy – *Reports and studies* – **The economic and financial situation in Belgium** – **No 4/93**

110 pp. * ECU 26 * ISSN 0379-0991 * CM-79-93-687-EN-C — 1993

Practical guide to legal aspects of industrial subcontracting within the European Community – Volume I – **The subcontract**

118 pp. * ECU 11.25 * ISBN 92-825-9593-5 * CB-27-89-001-EN-C — 1992

Practical guide to legal aspects of industrial subcontracting in the European Community – Volume II – **The legal framework of subcontracting in the twelve Member States**

70 pp. * ECU 9 * ISBN 92-826-4651-3 * CB-27-89-002-EN-C — 1992

The rules governing medicinal products in the European Community – Volume I – **The rules governing medicinal products for human use in the European Community** – *Revised edition / September 1991*

228 pp. * ECU 20 * ISBN 92-826-3166-4 * CO-71-91-631-EN-C — 1992

The rules governing medicinal products in the European Community – Volume II – **Notice to applicants for marketing authorizations for medicinal products for human use in the Member States of the European Community**

186 pp. * ECU 16.50 * ISBN 92-825-9503-X * CB-55-89-293-EN-C — 1992

The rules governing medicinal products in the European Community – Volume III – *Addendum No 2 – May 1992* – **Guidelines on the quality, safety and efficacy of medicinal products for human use**

206 pp. * ECU 23 * ISBN 92-826-4550-9 * CO-75-92-558-EN-C — 1992

The rules governing medicinal products in the European Community – Volume IV – **Good manufacturing practice for medicinal products**

177 pp. * ECU 19.50 * ISBN 92-826-3180-X * CO-71-91-760-EN-C — 1992

The rules governing medicinal products in the European Community – Volume VA – **The rules governing veterinary medicinal products in the European Community** – Revised edition/November 1992

218 pp. * ECU 24 * ISBN 92-826-5174-6 * CO-77-92-384-EN-C — 1993

The rules governing medicinal products in the European Community – Volume VI – Establishment by the European Community of maximum residue limits (MRLs) for residues of veterinary medicinal products in foodstuffs of animal origin

127 pp. * ECU 13.50 * ISBN 92-826-3173-7 * CO-71-91-768-EN-C — 1992

Credit institutions – Community measures adopted or proposed – *Situation as at August 1992*

356 pp. * ECU 37 * ISBN 92-826-4842-7 * C1-76-92-293-EN-C — 1992

Third survey on State aids in the European Community in the manufacturing and certain other sectors
84 pp. * ECU 10 * ISBN 92-826-4637-8 * CV-75-92-881-EN-C — 1992

Green Paper on the development of the single market for postal services (Communication from the Commission) – COM(91) 476 final
371 pp. * ISBN 92-77-45007-X * CB-CO-92-263-EN-C — 1992

Farm take-over and farm entrance within the EEC
148 pp. * ECU 15 * ISBN 92-826-3667-4 * CM-73-91-376-EN-C — 1992

Copyright and information limits to the protection of literary and pseudo-literary works in the Member States of the EC
262 pp. * ECU 27 * ISBN 92-826-3666-6 * CM-75-92-049-EN-C — 1992

Social security for persons moving within the Community – *Social Europe 3/92*
154 pp. * ECU 19 * ISSN 0255-0776 * CE-AA-92-003-EN-C — 1992

Urban social development – *Social Europe – Supplement 1/92*
125 pp. * ECU 9 * ISBN 92-826-4013-2 * CE-NC-92-001-EN-C — 1992

Towards a Europe of solidarity: housing – *Social Europe – Supplement 3/92*
142 pp. * ECU 9 * ISBN 92-826-4567-3 * CE-NC-92-003-EN-C — 1992

EUR 13914 – European cooperation in the field of scientific and technical research, COST secretariat with the assistance of J. L. Roland
93 pp. * ECU 16.50 * ISBN 92-826-4371-9 * CG-NA-13914-EN-C — 1992

EUR 14326 – The European market for value analysis
139 pp. * ECU 15 * ISBN 92-826-4130-9 * CD-NA-14326-EN-C — 1992

The current situation, evolution and future prospects for agriculture in Yugoslavia
128 pp. * ECU 12 * ISBN 92-826-3485-X * CM-72-91-899-EN-C — 1992

A practical guide to cross-border cooperation
112 pp. * ECU 10 * ISBN 92-826-3143-5 * CT-70-91-992-EN-C — 1992

New information technology in education – France
110 pp. * ECU 13 * ISBN 92-826-4771-4 * CY-03-92-007-EN-C — 1992

New information technology in education – Germany
124 pp. * ECU 13 * ISBN 92-826-4683-1 * CY-03-92-004-EN-C — 1992

New information technology in education – Denmark
138 pp. * ECU 14 * ISBN 92-826-4681-5 * CY-03-92-003-EN-C — 1992

New information technology in education – The Netherlands
108 pp. * ECU 12 * ISBN 92-826-4779-X * CY-03-92-011-EN-C — 1992

New information technology in education – Luxembourg
122 pp. * ECU 13 * ISBN 92-826-4777-3 * CY-03-92-010-EN-C — 1992

Removal of tax obstacles to the cross-frontier activities of companies – *Supplement 4/91 – Bull. EC*
67 pp. * ECU 4.25 * ISBN 92-826-3025-0 * CM-NF-91-004-EN-C — 1992

Agriculture in Europe
97 pp. * ECU 7 * ISBN 92-826-0476-4 * CM-60-90-418-EN-C — 1992

Telecommunications in Europe, Herbert UNGERER with the collaboration of Nicholas P. COSTELLO
Revised edition, 1990
257 pp. * ECU 10 * ISBN 92-826-1640-1 * CM-59-90-346-EN-C — 1992

European Economy – No 35 – The economics of 1992
222 pp. * ECU 16 * ISSN 0379-0991 * CB-AR-88-035-EN-C — 1992

European Economy – No 36 – Creation of a European financial area – Liberalization of capital movements and financial integration in the Community
212 pp. * ECU 16 * ISSN 0379-0991 * CB-AR-88-036-EN-C — 1992

European Economy – No 40 – Horizontal mergers and competition policy in the European Community
98 pp. * ECU 16 * ISSN 0379-0991 * CB-AR-89-040-EN-C — 1992

European Economy – No 45 – Stabilization, liberalization and devolution – Assessment of the economic situation and reform process in the Soviet Union
191 pp. * ECU 18 * ISSN 0379-0991 * CB-AR-90-045-EN-C — 1992

European Economy – No 50 – Annual Economic Report 1991-92 – Strengthening growth and improving convergence
285 pp. * ECU 20 * ISSN 0379-0991 * CM-AR-91-050-EN-C — 1992

European Economy – No 51 – The climate challenge – Economic aspects of the Community's strategy for limiting CO_2 emissions
253 pp. * ECU 23.50 * ISSN 0379-0991 * CM-AR-92-051-EN-C — 1992

European Economy – Social Europe – The impact of the internal market by industrial sector: the challenge for the Member States – *Special edition – 1990*
340 pp. * ECU 18 * ISBN 92-826-1818-8 * CM-59-90-887-EN-C — 1992

Social Europe 3/91 – Equal opportunities for women and men
202 pp. * ECU 18 * ISSN 0255-0776 * CE-AA-91-003-EN-C — 1992

Guide to the reform of the Community's structural Funds
104 pp. * ECU 11.25 * ISBN 92-826-0029-7 * CB-56-89-223-EN-C — 1992

The rights of working women in the European Community, Eve C. LANDAU
244 pp. * ECU 5.25 * ISBN 92-825-5341-8 * CB-43-85-741-EN-C — 1992

1992: the European social dimension, Patrick VENTURINI
119 pp. * ECU 9.75 * ISBN 92-825-8703-7 * CB-PP-88-B05-EN-C — 1992

Research on the 'cost of non-Europe' – Basic findings
Volume 1 – **Basic studies: Executive summaries**
　　　　578 pp. * ECU 53.25 * ISBN 92-825-8605-7 * CB-PP-88-B14-EN-C — 1992

Volume 2 – **Studies on the economics of integration**
　　　　652 pp. * ECU 57 * ISBN 92-825-8616-2 * CB-PP-88-C14-EN-C — 1992

Volume 3 – **The completion of the internal market:**
　　　　A survey of European industry's perception of the likely effects
　　　　309 pp. * ECU 25.50 * ISBN 92-825-8610-3 * CB-PP-88-D14-EN-C — 1992

Volume 4 – **The 'cost of non-Europe':**
　　　　Border-related controls and administrative formalities –
　　　　An illustration in the road haulage sector
　　　　280 pp. * ECU 22.50 * ISBN 92-825-8618-9 * CB-PP-88-E14-EN-C — 1992

Volume 5 (Parts A + B)
　　　　The 'cost of non-Europe' in public-sector procurement
　　　　Part A: 552 pp. * ISBN 92-825-8646-4 * CB-P1-88-F14-EN-C — 1992
　　　　Part B: 278 pp. * ISBN 92-825-8647-2 * CB-P2-88-F14-EN-C — 1992
　　　　Parts A + B: ECU 120 * ISBN 92-825-8648-0

Volume 6 – **Technical barriers in the EC: An illustration by six industries**
　　　　The 'cost of non-Europe': Some case studies on technical barriers
　　　　242 pp. * ECU 21 * ISBN 92-825-8649-9 * CB-PP-88-G14-EN-C — 1992

Volume 7 – **The 'cost of non-Europe': Obstacles to transborder business activity**
　　　　154 pp. * ECU 12.75 * ISBN 92-825-8638-3 * CB-PP-88-H14-EN-C — 1992

Volume 8 – **The 'cost of non-Europe' for business services**
　　　　140 pp. * ECU 13.50 * ISBN 92-825-8637-5 * CB-PP-88-I14-EN-C — 1992

Volume 9 – **The 'cost of non-Europe' in financial services**
　　　　494 pp. * ECU 120 * ISBN 92-825-8636-7 * CB-PP-88-J14-EN-C — 1992

Volume 10 – **The benefits of completing the internal market for telecommunication**
　　　　services equipment in the Community
　　　　197 pp. * ECU 17.25 * ISBN 92-825-8650-2 * CB-PP-88-K14-EN-C — 1992

Special price for the complete series: **ECU 360**

Commission of the European Communities
OFFICES

EIRE — IRELAND

Dublin

Commission of the European Communities
Office in Ireland

Jean Monnet Centre
39 Molesworth Street
Dublin 2
Tel. (353-1) 71 22 44
Fax (353-1) 71 26 57
Telex (0500) 93827 EUCO EI

UNITED KINGDOM

London

Commission of the European Communities
Office in the United Kingdom

Jean Monnet House
8 Storey's Gate
London SW1P 3AT
Tel. (44-71) 973 19 92
Fax (44-71) 973 19 00/19 10
Telex (051) 23208 EURUK G

Belfast

Commission of the European Communities
Office in Northern Ireland

Windsor House
9/15 Bedford Street
Belfast BT2 7EG
Tel. (44-232) 24 07 08
Fax (44-232) 24 82 41
Telex (051) 74117 CECBEL G

Cardiff

Commission of the European Communities
Office in Wales

4 Cathedral Road
Cardiff CF1 9SG
Tel. (44-222) 37 16 31
Fax (44-222) 39 54 89
Telex (051) 497727 EUROPA G

Edinburgh

Commission of the European Communities
Office in Scotland

9 Alva Street
Edinburgh EH2 4PH
Tel. (44-31) 225 20 58
Fax (44-31) 226 41 05
Telex (051) 727420 EUEDING

UNITED STATES OF AMERICA

Washington

Commission of the European Communities
External Delegation

2100 M Street, NW (Suite 707)
Washington DC 20037
Tel. (1-202) 862 95 00
Fax (1-202) 429 17 66
Telex (023) 64215 EURCOM NW

New York

Commission of the European Communities
External Delegation

3 Dag Hammarskjöld Plaza
305 East 47th Street
New York NY 10017
Tel. (1-212) 371 38 04
Fax (1-212) 758 27 18
Telex (023) 012396 EURCOM NY

JAPAN

Tokyo

Commission of the European Communities
External Delegation

Europa House
9-15 Sanbancho
Chiyoda-Ku
Tokyo 102
Tel. (81-3) 239 04 41
Fax (81-3) 239 93 37
Telex (072) 28567 COMEUTOK J

BELGIQUE/BELGIË
Bruxelles/Brussel
Commission des Communautés
européennes
Commissie van de Europese
Gemeenschappen
Bureau en Belgique/Bureau in België
Rue Archimèdestraat 73
B-1040 Bruxelles/Brussel
Tél.: (32-2) 295 38 44
Fax: (32-2) 295 01 66
Télex: 26657 COMINF B

DANMARK
København
Kommissionen for De Europæiske
Fællesskaber
Kontor i Danmark
Højbrohus
Østergade 61
Postbox 144
DK-1004 København K
Tlf.: (45-33) 14 41 40
Telefax: (45-33) 11 12 03/14 13 92
Telex: (055) 16402 COMEUR DK

FRANCE
Paris
Commission des Communautés
européennes
Bureau de représentation en France
288, boulevard Saint-Germain
F-75007 Paris
Tél.: (33-1) 40 63 38 00
Fax: (33-1) 45 56 94 17/18/19
Télex: (042) 202271F

Marseille
Commission des Communautés
européennes
Bureau à Marseille
2, rue Henri-Barbusse
F-13241 Marseille Cedex 01
Tél.: (33) 91 91 46 00
Fax: (33) 91 90 98 07
Télex: (042) 402538 EURMA

LUXEMBOURG
Commission des Communautés
européennes
Bureau au Luxembourg
Bâtiment Jean Monnet
Rue Alcide De Gasperi
L-2920 Luxembourg
Tél.: (352) 43 01
Fax: (352) 43 01 44 33
Télex: 3423/3446/3476 COMEUR LU

SUISSE/SCHWEIZ/SVIZZERA
Genève
Commission des Communautés
européennes
Bureau de presse et d'information
Kommission der Europäischen
Gemeinschaften
Presse- und Informationsbüro

Commissione delle Comunità europee
Ufficio stampa e informazione
Case postale 195
37-39, rue de Vermont
CH-1211 Genève 20 CIC
Tél.: (41-22) 734 97 50
Fax: (41-22) 734 22 36
Télex: (045) 414 165 ECOM CH

BR DEUTSCHLAND
Bonn
Kommission der Europäischen
Gemeinschaften
Vertretung in der Bundesrepublik
Deutschland
Zitelmannstraße 22
D-53113 Bonn 1
Tel.: (49-228) 53 00 90
Fax: (49-228) 530 09 50/12
Telex: (041) 886648 EUROP D

Berlin
Kommission der Europäischen
Gemeinschaften
Vertretung in der Bundesrepublik
Deutschland
Außenstelle Berlin
Kurfürstendamm 102
D-W-10711 Berlin 31
Tel.: (49-30) 896 09 30
Fax: (49-30) 892 20 59
Telex: (041) 184015 EUROP D

München
Kommission der Europäischen
Gemeinschaften
Vertretung in der Bundesrepublik
Deutschland
Vertretung in München
Erhardtstraße 27
D-80331 München 2
Tel.: (49-89) 202 10 11
Fax: (49-89) 202 10 15
Telex: (041) 5218135

ESPAÑA
Madrid
Comisión de las Comunidades
Europeas
Oficina en España
Calle de Serrano, 41, 5ª planta
E-28001 Madrid
Tel.: (34-1) 435 17 00
Telecopia: (34-1) 576 03 87/577 29 23
Télex: (052) 46818 OIPE E

Barcelona
Comisión de las Comunidades
Europeas
Oficina en España
Avenida Diagonal, 407 bis, 18ª planta
E-08008 Barcelona
Tel.: (34-3) 415 81 77
Telecopia: (34-3) 415 63 11
Télex: (052) 97524 BDC E

VENEZUELA
Caracas
Comisión de las Comunidades
Europeas
Delegación
Calle Orinoco, Las Mercedes
Apartado 67 076,
Las Américas 1061A
Caracas
Tel.: (58-2) 91 51 33
Telecopia: (58-2) 91 88 76
Télex: (031) 27298 COMEU VC

ΕΛΛΑΔΑ
Αθήνα
Επιτροπή των Ευρωπαϊκών
Κοινοτήτων
Γραφείο στην Ελλάδα
Βασιλίσσης Σοφίας 2
ΤΘ 30284
GR-10674 Αθήνα
Τηλ.: (30-1) 724 39 82/83/84
Τέλεφαξ: (30-1) 724 46 20
Τέλεξ: (0601) 219324 ECAT GR

ITALIA
Roma
Commissione delle Comunità europee
Ufficio in Italia
Via Poli, 29
I-00187 Roma
Tel.: (39-6) 699 11 60
Telecopia: (39-6) 679 16 58 / 679 36 52
Telex: (043) 610184 EUROMA I

Milano
Commissione delle Comunità europee
Ufficio a Milano
Corso Magenta, 59
I-20123 Milano
Tel.: (39-2) 48 01 25 05
Telecopia: (39-2) 481 85 43
Telex: (043) 316200 EURMIL I

NEDERLAND
Den Haag
Commissie van de Europese
Gemeenschappen
Bureau in Nederland
Korte Vijverberg 5
2513 AB Den Haag
Nederland
Tel.: (31-70) 346 93 26
Telecopie: (31-70) 364 66 19
Telex: (044) 31094 EURCO NL

PORTUGAL
Lisboa
Comissão das Comunidades
Europeias
Gabinete em Portugal
Centro Europeu Jean Monnet
Largo Jean Monnet, 1-10.°
P-1200 Lisboa
Tel.: (351-1) 350 98 00
Telecopiador: (351-1) 350 98 01/2/3
Telex: (0404) 18810 COMEUR P

ORDER FORM

European Economy   ISSN 0379-0991

Price annual subscription (2 issues and 3 reports per year):
ECU 90

European Economy + Supplements A and B

Price combined annual subscription:
ECU 135

Number
of copies:

....

....

Name and address:

Date: .... Signature: ....

ORDER FORM

Supplements to 'European Economy'.
Series A — **Recent economic trends**
Price annual subscription (11 issues per year):
ECU 37
Series B — **Economic prospects — business survey
results**
Price annual subscription (11 issues per year):
ECU 37
Price both supplements:
ECU 74

Number
of copies:

....

....

....

Name and address:

Date: .... Signature: ....

ORDER FORM

European Economy   ISSN 0379-0991

Price annual subscription (2 issues and 3 reports per year):
ECU 90

European Economy + Supplements A and B

Price combined annual subscription:
ECU 135

Number
of copies:

....

....

Name and address:

Date: .... Signature: ....

Office des
publications officielles
des Communautés européennes

L-2985 **Luxembourg**

Office des
publications officielles
des Communautés européennes

L-2985 **Luxembourg**

Office des
publications officielles
des Communautés européennes

L-2985 **Luxembourg**